Ask the Masters!

Ask the masters!

Organizing Your Scrapbook Supplies

From the Memory Makers Masters

Memory Makers Books
Cincinnati, Ohio
www.mycraftivity.com

Organizing Your Scrapbook Supplies. Copyright © 2008 by Memory Makers Books. Manufactured in China. All rights reserved. It is permissible for the purchaser to make the projects contained herein and sell them at fairs, bazaars and craft shows. No other part of this book may be reproduced in any form or by any electronic or mechanical means including information storage and retrieval systems without permission in writing from the publisher, except by a reviewer, who may quote a brief passage in review. Published by Memory Makers Books, an imprint of F+W Publications, Inc., 4700 East Galbraith Road, Cincinnati, Ohio 45236. (800) 289-0963. First edition.

12 11 10 09 08   5 4 3 2 1

Distributed in Canada by Fraser Direct
100 Armstrong Avenue
Georgetown, ON, Canada L7G 5S4
Tel: (905) 877-4411

Distributed in the U.K. and Europe by David & Charles
Brunel House, Newton Abbot, Devon, TQ12 4PU, England
Tel: (+44) 1626 323200, Fax: (+44) 1626 323319
E-mail: postmaster@davidandcharles.co.uk

Distributed in Australia by Capricorn Link
P.O. Box 704, S. Windsor, NSW 2756 Australia
Tel: (02) 4577-3555

Library of Congress Cataloging-in-Publication Data

Ask the masters! : organizing your scrapbook supplies. -- 1st ed.
    p. cm.
  ISBN 978-1-59963-030-4 (pbk. : alk. paper)
  1. Photograph albums--Equipment and supplies. 2. Photographs-
-Conservation and restoration. 3. Scrapbooking--Equipment and
supplies. I. Memory Makers Books (Firm)
  TR501.A84 2008
  745.593--dc22
                                2008020880

Metric Conversion Chart

to convert	to	multiply by
Inches	Centimeters	2.54
Centimeters	Inches	0.4
Feet	Centimeters	30.5
Centimeters	Feet	0.03
Yards	Meters	0.9
Meters	Yards	1.1
Sq. Inches	Sq. Centimeters	6.45
Sq. Centimeters	Sq. Inches	0.16
Sq. Feet	Sq. Meters	0.09
Sq. Meters	Sq. Feet	10.8
Sq. Yards	Sq. Meters	0.8
Sq. Meters	Sq. Yards	1.2
Pounds	Kilograms	0.45
Kilograms	Pounds	2.2
Ounces	Grams	28.3
Grams	Ounces	0.035

F+W PUBLICATIONS, INC.

Editors: Jessica Strawser, Eileen Aber, Christine Doyle
Content Editor: Darlene D'Agostino
Designer: Corrie Schaffeld
Art Coordinator: Eileen Aber
Production Coordinator: Greg Nock
Photographers: Tim Grondin, Richard Deliantoni
Stylists: Lauren Emmerling, Nora Martini, Jan Nickum

www.fwpublications.com

A Note from the Editor

When I first conceived the idea of making the third book in our Ask the Masters series one about organization, I knew it might be a little tricky. A little tricky to translate the great organization and storage ideas of our Memory Makers Masters into photographs. A little tricky to incorporate into an organization book the inspiring artwork we come to expect from our Memory Makers Masters. A little tricky indeed.

Well, it turned out to be even more than a little tricky. So tricky that it never would have come together at all without an amazing team effort, one greater than any other book I've worked on.

A huge part of that team, of course, was our Memory Makers Masters. Each year since 2003, we at Memory Makers have selected ten scrapbookers to inspire our magazine and book readers with their amazing creations. And with this book, we challenged them further to inspire us with their ideas for organizing and storing their scrapbook tools and supplies. True to form, they came through—big time. Their innovative solutions, their insights and their artwork make this book a must-have, whether your scrap space is a few feet of a cramped closet or a whole room all to yourself.

The other part of the team integral to the creation of this book was the dedicated freelancers and staff here at Memory Makers. Editors, writers, coordinators, designers, stylists and photographers who pooled all of their talents and worked within nutty schedules to create the photography and text included here.

It is therefore with great pleasure, and a big tip of my hat, that I present to you the third book in our Ask the Masters series, *Organizing Your Scrapbook Supplies*. I hope that it inspires you to not only organize your supplies but to use them in new and fabulous ways.

Enjoy!
Christine Doyle
Editorial Director, Memory Makers Books

TableofContents

Chapter Three | Materials   60

Chapter Four | Digital Supplies   98

Chapter Five | Masters Gallery   110

Introduction

They're baaaaaaack! Yep, the Masters have signed on for Round Three of super solid scrapbooking solutions. Only this time, it's personal. Actually, every time it's personal, because it's from the heart (awwww!). But this time, you're not only getting to peep fantastic artwork from the artists you love, you're getting a peek at their own creative spaces (prepare for some serious studio envy). This time, we're asking the Masters to help us get organized.

Let's face it—scrapbookers tend to accumulate not just a lot of stuff, but mounds, piles and stacks of it. Shopping for and collecting the product is half the fun of the hobby. But there needs to be order within your space if you're ever going to get any layouts finished (let alone, find your worktable and see the floor). Organizing can be a daunting task, but the first thing the Masters would like you to do is this: Turn that frown upside down and see how cool organizing can be. Organizing your scrap space will give you an opportunity to:

- Clear out the mental cobwebs and invite more creativity into your soul.
- Create more light and energy in your space.
- Help the environment by reusing, repurposing and recycling old supplies and odds and ends around the house that can be used in your new space.
- Come up with new layout ideas as you uncover products you forgot you had.
- Surprise yourself at your own ingenuity and interior design flair.

You want to be more relaxed, find more inspiration and be more productive, right? Right?! So, read this book, create a plan and begin to tackle it. Organization is not something you have to do in one weekend. Start with small steps and in no time you'll be queen of the clean. First you'll learn to organize the scrap space itself—from displaying your ideas and inspiration, to setting up an inviting scrap table or desk, to making the most of whatever storage space you have on hand. Then you'll be presented with the specifics: first, borrowing the Masters' clever ideas for corralling all of those tools into their own special homes (stamps and scissors and punches, oh my) so you can find them when you need them. Then you'll move on to getting that overflowing stash of materials under control: taming piles of untouched paper just waiting to be used, organizing even bigger piles of paper scraps accumulated from layouts gone by, and finding attractive yet handy ways to store every embellishment under the crop light. And of course we're living in a digital world, so no organizational guide would be complete without including computers and cameras. Those with unprinted and unlabeled (but not unloved) digital photos abandoned on CDs, flash drives, memory cards and hard drives, we're talking to you!

So, get comfortable because we're sure that by now you are enthralled with the contents of this book. And anytime the organizational crankies besiege your mind and make you want to halt what you are doing, just remember that you are taking an important first step toward becoming a better scrapbooker. Just because it's not that easy doesn't mean it can't be fun!

Meet the Masters

« Tracy Austin

What is your most innovative storage solution?

The "I'm-too-lazy-to-put-bits-away-properly catchall cleanup solution." If it is pulled for a project in mind and then subsequently goes unused, I have containers to shove all those scrappy leftovers. Be it buttons, embellishments or paper, they all have a place to be shoved for temporary storage because I know they just aren't going to ever find their way back home. Then, I dig in these spots first for my next project!

« Jodi Amidei

What tool or supply is always out of place?

For me, this would always be my craft knife and clear graphing ruler. I never scrap without these—they're the only way I get really even, straight cuts.

« Jessie Baldwin

What is your most innovative storage solution?

I have a six-drawer cart that I have labeled with different colors on the front. I put all my scraps in those drawers. It's great when I need something for card making or projects my kids are doing. I don't mind the kids getting into those drawers, because they are my scraps, and they love that they can use Mommy's scrapbook stuff.

« Iris Babao Uy

What part of your scrap space do you always keep neat and tidy?

That would be my table. I have this habit of cleaning up my table before starting a new layout. If I don't do that, I would not be able to find my way through all the mess.

« Valerie Barton

In what ways does your scrap space reflect your personal taste and style?

The colors reflect my personal taste, I love blues and greens together. It also reflects my style by looking like a well-decorated room, not just a scrap space or a scrapbook store. It's a room I'm proud to let people enter.

« Christine Brown

In what ways does your scrap space reflect your personal taste and style?

I think it reflects that I can be a hoarder and clutter bug. I have to work hard at purging and keeping things organized—otherwise, it quickly becomes cluttered.

« Susan Cyrus

What part of your scrap space do you always keep neat and tidy?

My pen jar stays nice and orderly. It's easier to remember to put the pen back in the jar than it is to sift through everything else on my desk to put it back.

« Sheila Doherty

What tool or supply is always in a pile or mess?

Everything! I'm a "piler." When I start working on a layout, I pull out all kinds of papers and embellishments that I would like to consider for that layout. They have a tendency to take over my workspace until I have barely enough room for my actual layout!

« Staci Etheridge

What is your most innovative storage solution?

I am a totally eclectic decorator—if I love it, it works for me! So my scrap room is filled with a mixture of new cost-effective storage (baskets, bins, etc.) and old, repurposed flea-market finds (doors, racks and more). Surrounding myself with bright, lively, happy things makes for a happy scrapper!

Meet the Masters

« Kathy Fesmire

In what ways does your scrap space reflect your personal taste and style?

I love my scrap space! It is so bright and colorful. The work wall is white, but the others are lime green and turquoise. Bright, colorful and loud—just like me! Since I love the colors in my room I tend to scrap those colors frequently, as well. I have projects and layouts displayed everywhere to remind me why I scrap: all the smiling faces looking back at me. I would say that my scrap space is more a reflection of me than any other room in my house.

« Catherine Feegel-Erhardt

When you scrap, are you a stander or a sitter?

I am a stander all the way—doesn't matter if it is a thirty-minute class or an eighteen-hour cropping marathon. There are two reasons why I am a stander. 1) With a deep breath, I am only five feet tall. If I sit to work, it feels like I am working uphill, and in most chairs my feet don't touch the floor. 2) Since turning forty my eyesight is clear only if the page is a good arm's length away—even with the trusty "readers" on.

« Diana Graham

What part of your scrap space do you always keep neat and tidy?

I always try to keep my photos neat, because if those are a mess I have to spend time sorting through stuff to get to what I really want to do, which is play with my scrapbooking materials.

« Kelly Goree

What tool or supply is always in a pile or mess?

My punches and my inks are just thrown into a bucket on my work surface as they are my most commonly used products. But I have to admit, I hate digging through them all to find what I want. So, inevitably, the bucket gets dumped on my work station until the project is through.

« Greta Hammond

What is your most innovative storage solution?

I love how I have stored my Cricut machine and many, many cartridges. I used to have to drag it out all the time and the cartridges were always tucked away and I couldn't tell what I had. Now it is always plugged in on a TV cart that rolls out from under a worktable. The cartridges are neatly lined up on the shelf below, easy to spot and pick out! I definitely use it more often because it is so easy to get to.

» HillaryHeidelberg

In what ways does your scrap space reflect your personal taste and style?

I am a simple scrapper, so I have a relatively small scrap space. Just an armoire and a 2' × 2' desk to scrap on. I don't stash a lot of embellishments or alphabets, as I simply don't have the room. Come to think of it, it's hard to figure out which came first: the small space or my simple style.

JenieceHiggins

What is your most innovative storage solution?

On my shelves I keep multiple baskets. I had fabric liners made for the baskets so that small pieces don't get lost in the basket weave (and they look pretty). I divide supplies by category into the baskets. I can reach many of them right from my desk. I like this system because it keeps everything handy and it makes for very easy cleanup.

» NicHoward

When you scrap, are you a stander or a sitter?

I do both. Mostly sitting, until things get serious—then I stand up to get a bird's eye view, sit down, stand up, walk to the pantry and stare in there for a while, sit down at the scrapping desk, stand up, walk to the mailbox, sit down—you get the picture!

» CarolineIkeji

What tool or supply is always in a pile or mess?

Patterned paper. I never, ever put it away after pulling it out, and it always ends up in a really huge pile. I try to organize it into some sort of system, but that system always ends up being abandoned as the pile grows bigger and bigger. I also tend to use only what's in the pile, as it's easy access.

» Brittany Laakkonen

When you scrap, are you a stander or a sitter?

I actually sit on the floor. I have done it for so long, I have a hard time scrapping standing up!

Meet the Masters

« Lisa Pace

In what ways does your scrap space reflect your personal taste and style?

I love anything and everything vintage, so I use old vases, bowls and jars bought in thrift shops to store some of my supplies. Large, clear pickle jars are perfect for holding ribbons, and old canning jars are one of my favorites for storing buttons. Old bowls of any kind keep my basic tools tidy and easy to reach.

« Amelia McIvor

What tool or supply is always in a pile or mess?

The supplies for whatever I am working on at the moment are always in a big pile. I start off with a nice clean work area, but as the page progresses, things that I am using or deciding between get pulled from their storage spots and piled high. That's everything in the one pile—paper, ribbon, alphas, stamps, markers!

« Amy Peterman

When you scrap, are you a stander or a sitter?

I like to do a little of both. That's why I chose to have a work surface that is counter height with a bar stool. That way, I can stand when I feel like it and not be hunched over, and sit when I feel like it (which is especially nice for journaling).

« Ronee Parsons

When you scrap, are you a stander or a sitter?

Both. I sit down for a while, and then I get antsy, so I get up and kind of walk around and think and then look at the piece from afar, then come back and sit down.

« Suzy Plantamura

What part of your scrap space do you always keep neat and tidy?

I try to keep my work desk organized and clean, as it drives me crazy to work in clutter. It gets completely piled up during a project or layout, but as soon as it is done, I completely clean it again so it is ready for the next one. I even use a magic eraser to get all the extra adhesive and marker or paint stains removed. I *must* work on a clean desk!

«TracieRadtke

What is your most innovative storage solution?

I store my rubber stamps in a big red decorative box that sits on top of my computer armoire. I don't think people realize that it's a functional piece versus a decorative piece.

«CrystalJeffrey Rieger

In what ways does your scrap space reflect your personal taste and style?

It definitely reflects me. There are bright splashes of color (mostly reds) and I have tried to make all my storage solutions easy to maintain. Otherwise, I know I will not keep it up. I am not the neatest of people, so I have learned my limitations and have tried to make the organization of my supplies easy to use and maintain so that it works for me. I like that my baskets allow me to toss things in when I tidy up and to dig in them when looking for something. Nothing feels like more work to me than trying to find an exact spot for everything. I am definitely a toss and go kind of girl.

«HeidiSchueller

In what ways does your scrap space reflect your personal taste and style?

I have a small space, so that helps keep everything close to me, but it also forces me to be clean because it's too small to mess up—I'd never find anything! I think by keeping my room inviting with my paints out, chipboard visable and papers all along the wall for me to see, it just screams CREATE!

«TorreyScott

What is your most innovative storage solution?

I store my dies in a zippered CD notebook. Each die goes in its own pocket, magnetically affixed to an index card that I lined with a strip of magnetic tape. This keeps them from falling out. The whole thing zips closed and has a handle for carrying.

«KatrinaSimeck

What tool or supply is always in a pile or mess?

Without a doubt, ribbon! I have jars that are perfectly organized, but then I have baskets and bins that are a train wreck.

Meet the Masters

≪ Shannon Taylor

In what ways does your scrap space reflect your personal taste and style?

I'm not a clutter girl! Most of my appliances in my kitchen are put away, and I'm the same with my scrap room. I'm not a neat freak by any means (just ask my hubby), but I don't like lots of stuff out.

≪ Michele Skinner

What is your most innovative storage solution?

I bit the bullet and sorted all my embellishments by color and type. Sometimes you just *know* a page needs a little red something, and instead of digging through all my stuff, I can now go straight to the red drawer. Genius. I wish I'd made the switch long ago.

≪ Denise Tucker

What part of your scrap space do you always keep neat and tidy?

My collections of eyelets are always stored neatly. I purchased multiple watch tins and cases to store them in. These items don't get used too often, so they manage to remain organized.

≪ Nicole Stark

What is your most innovative storage solution?

Keeping my ribbon in jars organized by color. I use my stash so much more now, and I love the effect of the jars lined up in the rainbow colors on my shelf above my work space.

« Lisa Tutman-Oglesby

What tool or supply is always in a pile or mess?

If anyone has a great storage idea for small rub-ons, I'm all ears. I generally have them all piled up on a paper plate on my craft island, but even that doesn't save them from sticking to each other and consequently getting tossed. Ugh!

« Samantha Walker

In what ways does your scrap space reflect your personal taste and style?

Personally, I like bargains, and I like to use and reuse things so that I don't have to spend more money. My scrap space is a hodge-podge of this and that—hand-me-downs from other rooms of the house and many great bargains to keep my costs down.

« Susan Weinroth

What tool or supply is always in a pile or mess?

My most-used punches—circle, corner rounder, square, and flower—are always in a pile on the corner of my desk. It just makes more sense to keep them out and handy rather than getting them out for almost every single project!

« Angelia Wigginton

What part of your scrap space do you always keep neat and tidy?

My tool caddy. After each scrapping session, I return my tools to my caddy, and my caddy to the same spot on my desk. The desk might be piled up and my ribbons in a tangle, but I can grab my caddy and scrapbook in another room, or be out the door to a friend's house to make cards with only a few minutes' notice.

« Holle Wiktorek

When you scrap, are you a stander or a sitter?

A rolling black leather chair works best for me! Curling up in my chair and rolling from my desk to computer, printer and other supplies equals relaxation. After chasing my toddler all day, my studio chair brings comfort and creativity.

Chapter One | Scrap Space

Scrapbooking is a serious art that needs serious space. Seriously! Whether you are lucky enough to have an entire room dedicated to your hobby or are a renegade scrapbooker seeking space wherever you can find it, now is the time to make your space work for you. First, you need to look at the big picture. Rather than getting bogged down with all the little details (my brads have teamed with my rhinestones and buttons, and they are systematically destroying my desktop organizer) take a deep breath and start thinking about your space as a whole. The goal: Create a room worth inviting creativity into instead of a mess you have to shut the door to every time company comes over. Or, transform a desk in the den: What was once the gathering place for junk mail and expired coupons can evolve into an efficient space where your creativity has room to flow. The Masters have been there, overcome that—and they're armed and ready with all the ideas you need to battle the forces conspiring against your organizational freedom.

Color me spoiled, but I have an entire room to dedicate to scrapbooking. When it comes to organizing it, color me clueless.

Having an entire studio can be as overwhelming as it is exciting. So, don't just set out to organize a room—set out to create a space. Your space. The goal is to create fun with function inside an atmosphere that fuel-injects your creativity. The first thing you should do is measure everything—the room, the closet, the furniture—and arrange the big pieces with efficiency in mind. Think about how you scrapbook. Where do you want your paper: to your left, to your right or perhaps in front of you? What supplies do you use most, and how can you incorporate them into your space so they'll be within arm's reach? Everyone is different, so check out some of the Masters' spaces for a few ideas.

Photo by Jessie Baldwin

⌃ JessieBaldwin

Some might affectionately call Jessie Baldwin a space hog. "People hate to have me over to scrap, and they hate to share tables with me at crops. My supplies tend to migrate until I have somehow encroached on all the surrounding area!" she says. In her own personal crop space, which for Jessie happens to be the room above her garage, work surfaces are a priority. "I spread out. Whatever space I have, I use it to the max . . . and then some." In the middle of the room is a large stainless steel table where she does most of her artwork and scrapbooking. She painted the walls a beautiful sky blue and adorned them with favorite photos and pieces of her artwork for constant inspiration. A quote—"Do What You Love"—painted on the wall keeps her motivated as she works. She stores her supplies in white cabinets she purchased from a local hardware store and assembled herself. You go, girl!

KatrinaSimeck »

Late-night scrapbookers would never get sleepy in a room as energetic as this—even if the room were tucked away in the basement. Katrina Simeck's brightly colored scrapbook space, painted cheery orange, green and white, is one such room. And it's perfect for keeping up with her late-night scrapping habit without waking her sleeping family. "I also have two large bulletin boards that serve as a home for inspirational photos, magazine clippings . . . pretty much anything that catches my eye. It's a really fun space!" Katrina keeps all of her supplies in the storage unit along the wall or in her newly organized closet, both within easy reach of the sturdy dining table where she works. "I take up a lot of space when I create! I usually have supplies strewn across my table or laid on the floor—it pretty much looks like a disaster by the time I'm finished."

Photo by Katrina Simeck

Photo by Greta Hammond

« GretaHammond

Super stylish and super functional. That's what Greta Hammond's scrap room is all about. On the style side, it's painted in warm colors that complement the lovely southern exposure that bathes the room. A big, chocolate brown chair sits next to the window with a standing invitation to get cozy while flipping through a book or magazine for inspiration. On the functional side, the room gets extra points for using space efficiently. "I love this work area because I made it extra deep (30" [76cm]) so I have plenty of space in front of me. It is an 'L' shape with my computer in the corner with a slide-out keyboard tray. I also have an island right behind me to hold larger tools like die-cutting machines, etc. The island has bookshelves on either end to hold baskets and boxes. I also have a large bookshelf on the opposite wall with cubes to hold vertical paper holders and other organizers."

Photo by Christine Brown

⌃ **Christine**Brown

When designing a room, why is it that we are too often tempted to shove a desk against the wall? We feel like we need to have that open space in the middle of the room for . . . for . . . for no other reason than just because. No more, says Christine Brown. She positioned her desk, actually an old conference table, perpendicular to the wall. "That way, I can use the wall space beside where I work for all of my essentials, and there is enough room for two people to scrap—one on either side." Christine converted a fourth bedroom on the first floor of her house into a scrap space full of personality. "My room is painted red! I love the color! It is so energizing and inspiring. I don't have a lot of wall space in my studio, but I did hang pretty white shelves above my desk and above my sewing machine to display some of my favorite projects."

ExpertAdvice!
What makes for a successful scrapbooking studio?

- Give everything a home sweet home. When every bit of your stash has a place to crash, you will spend more time crafting and less time searching for items you need. Lisa Tutman-Oglesby scraps by this rule, and you should, too.

- Admit it: You're messy. Once you accept the fact that you are going to make a mess of your scrap station, things will run more smoothly. Catherine Feegel-Erhardt keeps her work surface covered with a large piece of glass. This way she can wipe up paint and glue ickys easily. Katrina Simeck keeps her scrap table covered in white butcher paper. Not only does it make cleanup a breeze, it provides a surface she can sketch on if the urge arises.

- Put function first. A cute space is useless if not functional. Tracy Austin describes her space in three words: "Practical. Repurposed. Mine." She says her workspace is like a minivan: "Functional, practical, unpretentious and not in the least bit trendy or chic."

- Create your happy place. Kathy Fesmire made room for a mini fridge and reading chair in her scrap room, her ultimate retreat.

- Be a lean, clean, scrapbooking machine. Jodi Heinen keeps a designated space clear so she can evaluate her pages in progress for balance and symmetry without being distracted by the mess she made while creating the layout.

- Multitask like it's your job. Lisa Pace's studio includes several workstations, making multitasking a breeze. For example, while ink, paint or glue on one project is drying, she'll get busy adding stitching to another.

- Improvise. Iris Babao Uy lives in the Philippines, where organizational accessories for craft workspaces are not readily available. She improvises with kitchen organizers. Pretty much all of the her ideas in this book are a mark of her resourcefulness.

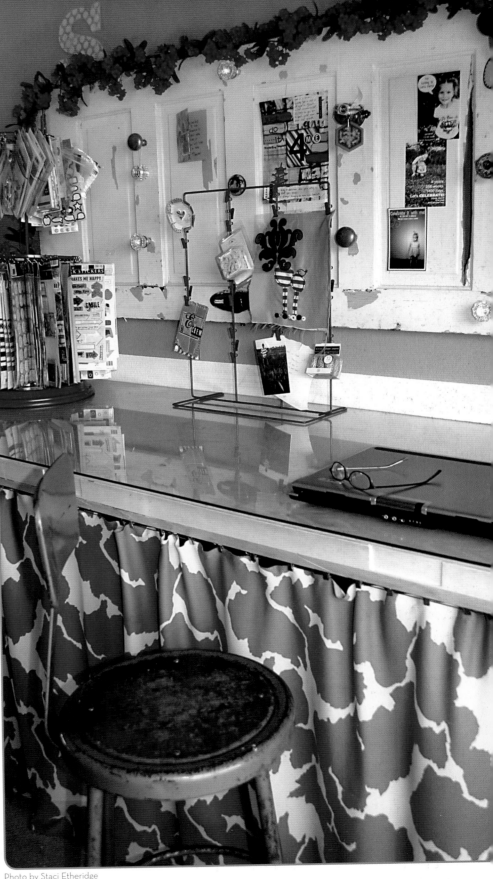

StaciEtheridge »

If you ask Staci Etheridge, formal dining rooms might be the most overrated
rooms in today's homes. Really, wouldn't
that space be more useful and have waaaay
more meaning if it were a dedicated scrap
space? So Staci converted her dining room
into a scrap haven. "It's perfect because
the windows overlook the backyard, so I
get lots of light and can see the kids if they
are playing in the yard. And since the room
was designed to hold a nice long table, I
was able to fit a good-sized desk so I can
spread out." The décor is vintage/eclectic,
and the room is lined with cabinets filled
with paper portfolios, tools and embellishments. "I'm also big on hiding my clutter.
I want my organization to be pretty and
interesting." But when work is in progress?
"I like to pull out whatever papers and
embellishments I am considering using and
spread them all around. The visual effect
of seeing everything I could potentially use
inspires me. Then I just play until I see what
speaks to me."

Photo by Staci Etheridge

Color me jealous: I haven't a clue where I can even put a worktable. A little help?

Not every Master has a fairy princess scrap room. Most Masters are like most people—space is at an absolute premium in the home. Many of them dedicate space in communal areas of their home: the rec room, the dining room, the family room, closets even. Whether your scrap space is in a guest room or inside a nook off your kitchen, it can still be your haven, your place to escape for hours of reprieve while getting lost in the world of color and images. But how? Let's ask the Masters.

⌃ **Tracie**Radtke

Tracie Radke could be a superhero scrapbooker. At first glance of the above photo, we see a contemporary family room, complete with a furry companion. But blink and look again (at right), and this scrapbooker's bat cave is revealed. "I suppose I am a minimalist when it comes to my scrap space," Tracie says. "My computer is inside an armoire along the wall between our family room and kitchen. My supplies are stored in a rolling cart and buffet along the same wall. When doing a digital layout, I need only my computer. When working with paper, I tend to just spread it out on the floor by my desk."

Photos by Tracie Radtke

This was our first year to offi-
cally trick-or-treat as city
people . Things are definitely
different. We trick-or-treated at
businesses rather than homes.
We also went out much earlier,
3:00pm-ish versus after dinner
like we had done in Texas. The
one thing that was the same...
LOTS AND LOTS OF CANDY!!

This year we went out trick-or-
treating twice. The first time
we went to Southport the
Sunday before Halloween with
Mallery, Azra and Amira. On
Halloween we went to the
nursing home and Broadway
with Cami, Celie and
Emma. Halloween
in the city is definitely
a good time!

minnie

TRICK
OR
TREAT

Minnie
by Tracie Radtke

Short on space? Why not give
hybrid scrapbooking a try? While
the base of this layout is digital, a
few well-placed traditional embellishments make it shine.

*Supplies: Digital storyboard template (We
Are Storytellers); letter template
by Lisa Whitney (ScrapArtist);
dotted paper by Weeds+Wildflowers
(Prima); red paper by Emily
Powers (We Are Storytellers); digital felt flower by Lili (ScrapArtist);
felt flowers (Prima); stamp (Hero
Arts); Misc: AL Uncle Charles
font, buttons, paint, ribbon*

ExpertAdvice!
My home is crowded to the max. How can I make it work?

- Encourage family participation. In the room where Valerie Barton does her scrapping, there's also a sofa and ottoman so the kiddos can hang out while Mom scraps. Everyone wins: Valerie can keep an eye on the little ones, and they can get their hands messy and make crafts of their own if the mood strikes. Jeniece Higgins also has a shared workspace—a long desktop with spots for three seats so her kids can join in the fun.

- Reconsider existing uses for furniture. Kelly Goree's deep freezer lived an unassuming life until the day she realized the large, wide top would make a great spare work surface. So, she cozied up her scrap station next to the deep freeze, and since then things have been anything but chilly.

- Scrap wherever you can. Angelia Wigginton scraps on her bed, in the serenity of her room. While her husband never complains of crumbs in the bed, he has woken up with eyelets stuck to the side of his face.

- Hide. People can and do scrapbook in New York City apartments. Hillary Heidelberg has a fold-down workspace that she can put away when not in use, kind of like a Murphy bed.

- Find a nook or cranny. Michele Skinner has no fear of dust bunnies or what lurks in the darkness. She scraps in her basement and utilizes the space under her stairs—complete with built-in storage cubbies—for storing all her papers (turn to page 26 to see more of her workspace).

Photo by Michele Skinner

⌃ **Michele**Skinner

Blend in, be inconspicuous, and no one will even know you're there. These are the tenets of Michelle Skinner's dedicated scrapbook space. She utilizes this multi-drawer work table to store all of her embellishments, adhesives, letter stamps and paper scraps. Perfect for keeping everything organized, yet out of sight. Also tucked in the corner of her finished basement is organizational furniture that matches the room's décor. "There are black-and-white framed photos around the space, so in my corner I have black-framed organizational components on the wall to blend with the surrounding space." Her family hardly notices she's taken up a significant portion of the room, and she can enjoy her hobby while spending time with her loved ones.

Escape

by Lisa Tutman-Oglesby

For Lisa, whose dedicated scrap space was a long time coming, creating a layout to her crafting haven just made sense. In the hidden journaling, she writes, "Whatever reason when I walk into this special space late at night, I'm in another world where I can relax and wind the stress of life down a notch or two, and maybe in the process, if I'm lucky, I can create something beautiful...that is if no one upstairs wakes up."

Supplies: Cardstock; die-cut shapes, patterned paper, transparent frame (My Mind's Eye); chipboard letters, photo corner (Heidi Swapp); sticker accent (Autumn Leaves); Misc: chipboard phrase

LisaTutman-Oglesby »

If you need to motivate your family to give you some much-deserved dedicated scrapbook space, try this tactic from Lisa Tutman-Oglesby: Stash your scrapbook supplies *everywhere*. "After years of pulling supplies out of kitchen cabinets, laundry room shelves and from under spare beds, we finally finished our basement with the express intention of retiring all crafting supplies to its own space," she says triumphantly. "My workspace and craft area occupies about half of the basement area, but my ultimate goal is to one day claim the entire basement as my own." Until her dreams of manifest destiny are realized, she is content to work in the basement at a large kitchen island (yep, just like the one in her kitchen where she used to stash some of her supplies). Lisa prefers to stand while scrapbooking, so this a perfect solution for her.

Photo by Lisa Tutman-Oglesby

? How do I conquer the chaos to start organizing *all* my stuff?

When it comes to getting organized, Masters of scrapbooking can also be the Masters of excuses. "I need the chaos to be creative." "If I organize, I won't know where everything is." "Some of my best layouts have been borne from a pile on my desk." "Getting organized means spending money on fancy-schmancy stuff." Get over it! Everyone can be organized—you just have to commit to taking the first step. Trust us, you'll be thankful that you did. Whether you buy a system specifically designed for organizing these types of supplies or create one of your own, the Masters agree that there's no right or wrong way as long as your way ultimately works for you.

Photo by Crystal Jeffrey Rieger

« CrystalJeffreyRieger

Know thyself. This is critical when it comes to determining exactly how you are going to systematically organize your stuff. For instance, some people must have everything in its right place. So, for them, drawers and file folders make sense. For Crystal Jeffrey Reiger (and maybe the rest of us), storing supplies in open bins works better. "I hate having to spend time putting things in a particular place—it takes away from my enjoyment," she says. "Cleanup is always done after each page is complete, but it is super fast because I just toss everything into its appropriate container. Basically, I have come to terms with the fact that I am messy and need low-maintenance ways to organize my stuff."

IrisBabaoUy »

You like to scrapbook because you're creative, right? Well, infuse a little bit of that sassafrass into organizing by gettin' all crafty. The beautiful and eclectic organization system in Iris Babao Uy's studio is the product of situational circumstances. She lives in the Phillippines, where the home organizational products available in the United States are not. So, she enjoys putting on her improviser hat. This wooden house is a great example. She uses it to hold lots of bottled product that's stored upright—and the top of the house comes off for easy access to her whole stash. But what makes it special is that she decorated it in her own style.

Photo by Iris Babao Uy

Photo by Staci Etheridge

« StaciEtheridge

Who doesn't like a good bargain? Staci Etheridge is quite the huntress when it comes to finding interesting secondhand pieces. Her scrap space consists of flea-market finds and vintage furniture. She calls this her "favorite lucky-find cabinet," which is filled with an assortment of smaller makeshift organizers: baskets, binders, boxes, crates and other odds and ends. Clear cabinet doors help her find what she needs at a moment's notice.

? What are some general storage solutions that are as pretty as they are functional?

Incorporating sassy storage solutions into the overall look and feel of your space has many benefits. First, it looks cute. Second, it keeps your stuff where you can see it, making it more likely that you will use it. Third, you get points for creatively utilizing space. And you get the chance to reuse, repurpose and recycle, whether that is in the form of giving a cool, new life to unused containers around the house or items within your scrap stash.

Photo by Jessie Baldwin

« JessieBaldwin

Jesse Baldwin puts the pretty in practical. For saving room on a crowded desktop, she loves these too cute metal buckets from IKEA (Eye-key-yah . . . sounds like Swedish for "cool"). They hang on the wall above her desk and keep scissors, pens and adhesives within arm's reach while minimizing desktop clutter.

IrisBabaoUy »

Ever the re-purposer, Iris uses a mug tree to store her favorite sticker and rub-on sheets in a fun and funky display. She simply ties a piece of ribbon to a clip, secures it to the top of a packet and hangs it out in plain sight. You can adapt this idea to hold virtually anything you don't mind storing out in the open.

Photo by Iris Babao Uy

TracyAustin »

Tracy Austin has what you could call a "creative buffet" on her desk—her most well-loved and well-used materials sit inside what she calls "quick-grab" baskets atop her desk, which is in a sunroom-turned-studio just off her bedroom. Among the essentials she keeps at the ready are adhesives, pens, scissors, photos and craft knives. She also keeps a pretty bowl on her desk to hold any "crumbs" that don't get put away.

Photo by Tracy Austin

Santa Wishes

by Tracy Austin

Raiding her bowl of pretty, leftover bits, Tracy spied these pieces of cardstock and found them to be the perfect addition to her layout. She ran the crumbled pieces of cardstock through her adhesive machine to easily adhere them.

Supplies: Cardstock; brad, patterned paper (KI Memories); chipboard letters (Heidi Swapp); letter stickers (American Crafts); sticker accents (American Crafts, KI Memories, Making Memories, Scenic Route); sequins (Doodlebug, Queen & Co.); pin (Fancy Pants); button (Autumn Leaves); flower (Doodlebug); Misc: paint

«LisaPace

If you are the rare type of scrapbooker who can honestly work neatly, then desktop organizers might work for you (they could also work if you are the opposite but have a really big desk, like, reaaaally big, really). Lisa Pace is the former. Get this: She has a spare bedroom in her house designated as a studio, yet she says she doesn't need much room. "As long as I have a 12" x 12" (30cm × 30cm) square I am set. I like to work in a small, contained area. Not sure why, but it just gets my creativity flowing." With so much space to spare, Lisa chooses desktop containers that suit her—vintage candy dishes to hold her most often-used supplies right out in the open.

Photo by Lisa Pace

Jewel Tea Co.

by Lisa Pace

Vintage pearl buttons are a favorite of Lisa's, so she keeps them in a clear jar near her workspace. That way, they're at the ready for pretty layouts like this one.

Supplies: Patterned paper (American Crafts, Making Memories); chipboard letters (Maya Road); buttons (Melissa Frances); ribbon (EK Success); crackling medium (DecoArt); Misc: floss, flowers, lace, paint, photo corners, tags, vintage postcard

JessieBaldwin »

Scrapbookers just should not have junk drawers. Scrapbookers with junk drawers end up with lost and forgotten supplies. Jessie Baldwin knows this and has found that even in her spacious and stylish scrap room, no matter how organized you get, you always end up with a bunch of supplies that can be classified only as "miscellaneous." Her solution is to display them in an overflowing old metal lunch box—a perfect way to prevent them from going the way of other misfit supplies.

Photo by Jessie Baldwin

Photo by Suzy Plantmura

« SuzyPlantamura

Mirror, mirror on the wall, who has the prettiest supplies of them all? Scrapbookers? Really? Oh, mirror! Inside Suzy Plantamura's scrap space, which is a former guest room turned country cottage-style studio, she puts her pretty supplies on display despite the fact that she delights in plenty of other storage space. She lined these pretty white shelves with jars filled with sorted embellishments for an out-in-the-open organizational solution that doubles as wall décor.

Photo by Christine Brown

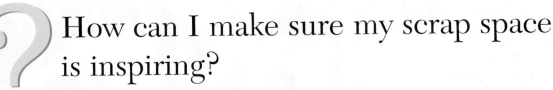

How can I make sure my scrap space is inspiring?

You are a scrapbook artist and, as such, you need a gallery. After all, it's the finished pieces that keep you going, that inspire you to create more and more pages, right? And pieces that have just been finished are simply too new and too good to place in an album right away. Displaying your artwork in your studio or around your home will keep you motivated and will earn you well-deserved kudos from friends and family. Pair it with other creative fodder, and you have a space ripe for inspired scrapping. Endless possibilities exist for putting your inspiration on display—and even storing up bonus creativity for later.

⌃ MasterSolution

Show us a Master without an inspiration board, and we'll show you a scrapbooker without a paper addiction. Inspiration boards come in all shapes and sizes, are readily store-bought and are easily handmade. The fabric-covered board shown here is an alternative to an ordinary bulletin board, but inspiration in the form of a favorite card, photo or piece of artwork is still just a thumbtack away. Magnetic boards work just as well, and many double as dry-erase boards you can use to sketch notes to yourself right where you can see them.

« ChristineBrown

A lack of wall space is no excuse not to display your finished scrapbook art. Christine Brown doesn't have a lot of wall space in her studio, so she found a shelf that was high on utility and low on space consumption (and, yay, it's pretty too!). Her favorite layouts can sit atop the shelf as well as hang below it from dainty decorative ribbons.

Friends for Life

Hanging out with the girls can literally help you live longer. Find out nine more ways to stay healthy. ⟩⟩⟩

FEEL AMAZING TODAY ⟫ NEWS YOUR BODY CAN REALLY USE

⌃ Caroline Ikeji

Is there a such thing as too many inspiration boards? Caroline Ikeji doesn't think so. "I have the back of a bookshelf facing my work area, so I tape up random inspiring pages out of magazines. I also have a bulletin board on the opposite side of the room, where I tape up random things—cool stuff that people have sent me, and random notes and pictures and ticket stubs." Of course, when it comes to inspiration boards, there's always room for one of those finished layouts that are too pretty to hide away, too.

Photos by Caroline Ikeji

NSSN
by Caroline Ikeji

In this layout, Caroline treats her postcard like a photo and her ticket like she would any patterned paper. With this approach, she's able to create a layout full of memorabilia that still looks fun and cohesive.

Supplies: Patterned paper (Paper Source); letter stickers, photo corners (American Crafts); die-cut shapes (Sassafras Lass); chipboard star (Li'l Davis); labels (Scenic Route); paper trim (Doodlebug, K&Co.)

Christine & Ryan
by Caroline Ikeji

The cute designs and embellishments from digital kits can serve as inspiration, too, so don't keep them filed away on your hard drive. Print out a few favorites and tack them on your inspiration board. Here, Caroline printed the digital brushes onto paper and adhered them to cardstock for an easy hybrid layout.

Supplies: Cardstock; letter stickers, photo corners (American Crafts); rhinestones (Target); digital brushes and kit by Anna Aspnes (Designer Digitals); digital frame by Katie Pertiet (Designer Digitals)

« StaciEtheridge

Talk about inspired. Staci Etheridge turned an old, unused door into a one-of-a-kind inspiration board. She covered it with miscellaneous doorknobs for an eclectic and functional touch—she can use the doorknobs to hang heavier items on the board. Brilliant! It's an idea that's ambitious to re-create, but you can put your own spin on it, as shown here, by merely attaching some corkboard to the panel on your own studio door or closet door. Decorative and useful!

The E*Crew
by Staci Etheridge

If you tack a great photo on an inspiration board, it's only a matter of time until you can't resist the urge to use it in an equally inspiring layout. This photo had such a great bright blue background that it begged for complementary-colored patterned paper.

Supplies: Patterned paper (7gypsies, Creative Imaginations); letter (Making Memories); sticker accents (EK Success, KI Memories, Martha Stewart); labels (Dymo); die-cut shapes (CherryArte); chipboard accents (Provo Craft); Misc: paint

Golf, Hawaii Style
by Amelia McIvor

Journals are another place to house inspiration for your next layout. Here, Amelia took the journaling in the corner of this page directly from a journal she kept during her trip to Hawaii.

Supplies: Cardstock; lace cardstock (KI Memories); letter clips, patterned paper (Making Memories); chipboard letters (Zsiage); rub-ons (Heidi Grace); Misc: Koala font, floss, paper flowers

Photo by Holle Wiktorek

⌃ **Holle**Wiktorek

No inspiring scrap space would be complete without some idea books or magazines. In Holle Wiktorek's scrap space (which she fondly calls "Studio H") the walls are tan, all the furniture and shelves are white and all the storage accessories are black. So these black plastic magazine files, which hold all her favorite publications right next to her notebooks and supplies, fit right in. She covered the clear openings in the sides with coordinating patterned paper and made labels for each file. When creative block strikes, she knows just where to go to coax the mojo into flowing again.

MAJ Promotion

by Holle Wiktorek

Photos courtesy U.S. Air Force

Holle's husband is a soldier and the son of a retired Army Major, so there are a lot of military experiences for Holle to scrap. Luckily, Studio H has plenty of room to store albums of touching layouts like this one.

Supplies: Cardstock; chipboard letters and star, patterned paper (Die Cuts With A View); ribbon (Offray); brads (Creative Impressions); labels (Dymo); die-cut tab (QuickKutz); Misc: Challenge font, hole punch, ink

ExpertAdvice!

What's *the* best way to store finished scrapbook albums?

Survey says: No one could agree. Some like to keep their albums away from humanity, while others want to share them at all costs. Here is a list of tips compiled from the Masters' responses. Follow the advice that works for you, but above all, keep those babies in good condition.

• Iris Babao Uy stores all of her albums in fabric bags to protect them from dust.

• Valerie Barton recommends storing them upright so the heavy embellishments on some pages don't weigh down any of the other layouts.

• Samantha Walker keeps her scrapbooks in her guest room, where the guests are usually close family members. "I tell our guests they are welcome to flip through the scrapbooks if they want to. That way, they don't feel obligated to look, and they don't feel snoopy if they want to look, because I've given them permission."

• Holle Wiktorek and Lisa Pace also keep albums in baskets out in the open, where guests can look through them.

? What if the space I'm scrapping in is not my space at all? Is it possible to be organized for cropping on the go?

Packing is a challenge for most of us. Especially for short trips. Wouldn't it be nice and easy to have one reasonably sized bag that you can carry (and actually lift) on the plane? It would have only what you need and not a camisole more. To make this dream a reality in your scrapbooking life, all you need is a good bag and some good old-fashioned planning. The key is to give yourself time to pack. Rushing will only cause you to forget something, damage supplies and lay waste to your newly organized studio. You will also have the tendency to overpack, throwing unnecessary stuff into a disorganized mess. Luckily, Masters are pros when it comes to scrapping on the go, and full of good ideas for mobile organization and creativity.

« MasterSolution

Don't let this be you: "I remember the first crop I went to and I showed up with everything! Literally everything! I made four trips to my car to get the four huge Rubbermaid bins . . . you know, the kind you store Christmas décor in?" This is the story of Catherine Feegel-Erhardt, who has since streamlined her cropping on the go with a crop bag. Expensive, perhaps, but bags designed specifically for crops are the choice of most of the Masters (it's hard to admit, but that birthday does roll around every year . . . the chance of receiving a sweet crop bag might make turning another year older tolerable). Scrapbooking has evolved to the point that bag designers have pretty much thought of everything. Crop bags are equipped with compartments for everything you can imagine bringing with you, and they often have wheels for easy traveling.

AngeliaWigginton »

Planner types get a bad rap. More "care-free," less organized people think planners are stiff, but in reality, it's the planner who experiences less frustration and anxiety. Angelia Wigginton will tell you that the secret to carefree cropping on the go is preplanned page kits like the ones shown here. "They lighten your load *and* allow you to get the most from your cropping time," she says. "You can put a variety of supplies in the kit for flexibility (stickers, ribbon) and by packing your basic elements, you'll be able to create pages without feeling like you have to dig through a mountain of scrapbook supplies. And, when you get home, you don't have nearly as much to unpack and put away."

« **Sheila**Doherty

Head to a crop without a plan, and guess where you'll go? Nowhere fast. It will be like your high school study group. You get together with your crop mates with the intention of starting on your project, only the temptation to chat will transform your love of scrapbooking into dreaded home-work. You won't know where to start or what you want to say about your photos. Suddenly, it's midnight, and you've barely picked out your patterned papers. Ugh! You can prevent this by journaling about your photos or sketching the layouts you plan to make before you go, says Sheila Doherty. If you have a plan, you can chat and crop. No sweat.

YOU ASKED FOR IT! NEW COLUMN
Mem
SCRAPBOOKING
Meet the NEW MASTERS!
PLUS:
scrapbook
page|maps
photo

« Tracy Austin

Tracy Austin recommends carrying your supplies to local crops in a laundry basket. For real. It's cheap, it's a good size and weight, and it's plastic, so you don't have to worry about leaky adhesives, paints or inks ruining an expensive bag. Plus, look how much stuff fits in the example shown here. It's way more fun than a load of whites!

Master Solution »

Scrapbooking is such a crafting playground—so many techniques and products to use. Creativity can travel in countless directions. That's why it's so hard for the traveling cropper to limit herself. When Katrina Simeck crops on the road, she tries to confine all of her supplies to a backpack. "It's much lighter, and the smaller space forces me to really think about what I'm packing," she says. Lots of other Masters also recommend keeping a spare tool kit (like the one shown here) packed and ready to go at a moment's notice. That way, you're sure not to forget anything you absolutely need. And who likes to be that cropper? You know, that cropper who keeps stealing, I mean, borrowing everyone's adhesive and craft knives *all night long.*

Expert Advice!
What are some other secrets for cropping success?

- Work smart, not hard. If scrapping at a crop is just too much of an organizational stress for you or too distracting of an environment for you to be creative, Tracy Austin recommends you bring along finished pages and assemble them into an album instead. Holle Wiktorek recommends going to a crop simply to watch and learn techniques and ideas from fellow scrappers. You could also spend your crop time making smaller elements, such as tags, frames and cards.

- Be prepared. If you live by the mantra, "have scrapbooking supplies, will travel," Diana Graham recommends keeping a grab-and-go basket of your scrap essentials in your car so you're always ready at a moment's notice.

- Don't mess with success. Since Greta Hammond's studio is so impeccably organized, she takes items in the containers she stores them in. That way, when she gets home, she just puts the whole container (or drawer) back where it belongs. Nic Howard also only takes things with her that can be placed back on the shelf. "I don't take things out of containers to take with me. I take the whole container or not at all."

Chapter Two | Tools

If only it were as easy as a tool belt or toolbox. Actually, it can be. Just ask the Masters. All it takes to organize your tools is a little thought. First, you need to place them in a hierarchy. Place your basic tools—used for almost every layout—at the top. Those you use quite frequently follow, and tools you use infrequently (Fourth of July-themed paper punch, anyone?) come last. Then it's a matter of figuring out how much you have of each so you may properly store them with adequate space.

Once you've prioritized and determined storage needs, you'll need to think about *how* you will use each tool. This will be the key to figuring out where to put it. Obviously, basics need to be within reach. For the tools you use frequently, you may want to consider organizing an area dedicated to them (e.g., a stamping station). Rarely used tools can occupy the tops of shelves or boxes under the bed. Anywhere but prime scrapbooking real estate will do.

It's a dirty job, but somebody's got to do it, and we promise you that once you see how much these solutions maximize your workspace as well as your productivity, you'll be glad you did!

Figuring out an efficient way to organize my basic tools is beyond me. How do you do it?

Part of the problem with organizing basic tools is figuring out what your basic tools really are and where they should be in relation to your work surface. Think of an office desk: The basics would be your pens, pencils, scissors, stapler and tape. Often, these supplies are kept within easy reach. Notice, the supplies are few. As a scrapbooker, your basic supplies are scissors, a ruler, a few favorite pens, a craft knife and extra blades, as well as a few signature items for your personal brand of scrapbooking. Make a list of your ten most-loved tools, then figure out the best way to store them.

« Samantha Walker

Samantha Walker's basement scrap studio is like a heaven, but instead of clouds, tables surround this angel. "I have a table that is dedicated to die-cutting stuff, a table dedicated to cutting and stamping stuff, another table to spread stuff out on, another table for sewing, some tables that serve dual purposes. Sometimes my area gets really crazy and even with all this table space, I end up scrapping in my lap!" OK, so she has a somewhat expanded definition of "basics." But she does have a great idea we all can use with her mighty pegboard. It's where all her handiest tools can hang out (ha ha), right where she can see them. It saves table space as well as time spent hunting through drawers.

Photo by Samantha Walker

Photo by Suzy Plantamura

⌃ SuzyPlantamura

Some folks are naysayers when it comes to the scrapbooker's toolbox. Look, we're not asking you to fit everything inside of it, just the basics. It will be so handy that you'll hardly be able to stand it! Suzy Plantamura favors this method because the stacked drawers make it easy to organize the tried-and-true items she needs in her scrapbooking arsenal. There's plenty of space for a ruler, hammer, jaw pliers, brayer, tweezers, stylus, eyelet setter and heat tools. As an added bonus, she is ready to grab and go when the occasion arises.

Jordan Turns 22

by Suzy Plantamura

All good layouts start with the basics, and Suzy put them to use in this layout before adding a finishing touch of shine. To get this same look, cut circles from white cardstock and spray glimmer mist, then apply embossing powder while the mist is still wet. Use your heat tool to melt the embossing powder. So easy!

Supplies: Cardstock; chipboard arrow and numbers, ribbon (Maya Road); trim (BasicGrey); circle template (Fancy Pants); glimmer mist (Tattered Angels); embossing powder (Ranger); Misc: heat tool, pen

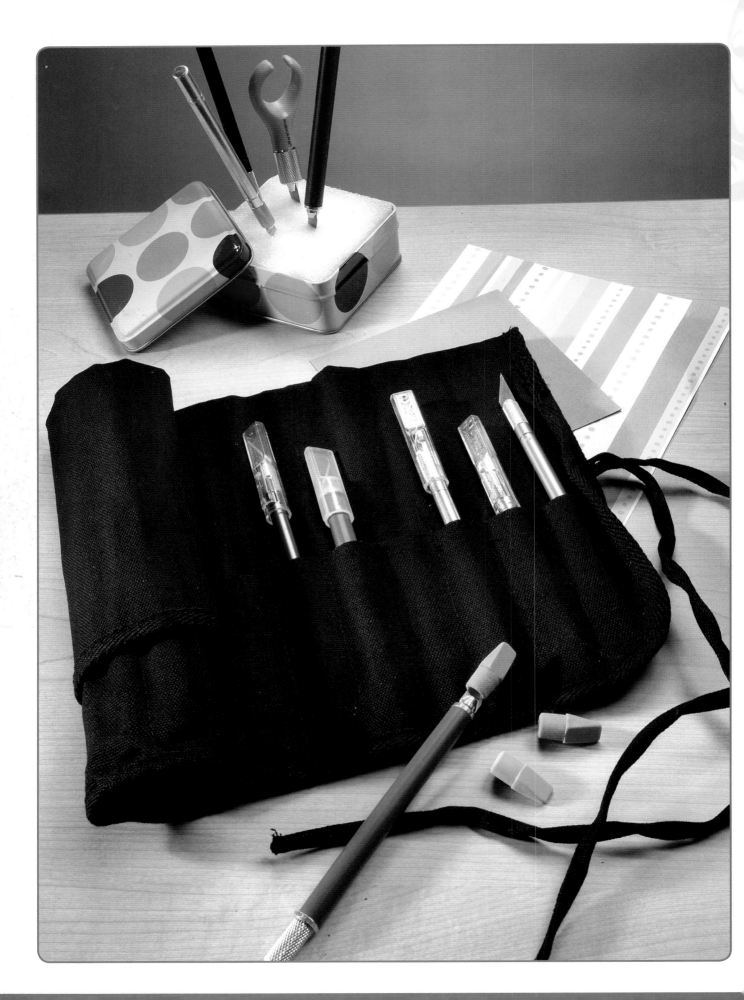

? I'm not the sharpest when it comes to organizing cutting tools. Please save me a trip to the emergency room.

Cutting tools make up a healthy slice of your tool arsenal—and if you have curious little ones, pets or clumsy husbands in the house, they can pose a safety threat, too. If casually left on your work surface, they can even threaten you (think cutting blades or sharp points hidden under strewn paper or how ouchie it would be if your craft knife rolled off the table and onto your foot). Every scrapbooker needs a go-to cutting-tool solution that is within easy reach. But a few of our motivated Masters took it a bit further.

« MasterSolution

Amelia McIvor has her own version of a "carpenter's belt" that she wears around her waist when she's crafting. Not only does this method allow for easy access while she works, it keeps sharp scissors and knives safe from little hands and makes for easy storage, too—simply roll it up and put it away. And the Masters were filled with other ideas for staying safe. If you've lost the cover that protects a craft knife, you can still store it safely in the pouch: Simply plug that pointy head into a basic eraser tip. Looking for a time-saver? While you're working, if taking all those LIDS on and off is too much of a hassle, simply keep a Styrofoam ball on hand where you can stick the knives in between cuts.

LisaPace »

If you have the space and the creativity to spare, just about anything can look good on display. Lisa Pace stores her collection of decorative scissors in pretty white vases. This makes for easy access that's just as charming as it is handy.

Photo by Lisa Pace

S

by Nicole Stark

Now that you know where they are, put your scissors to use creating custom-shaped pattern paper. To get the look Nicole has here, trace the scallops from an existing border, then cut out the pattern. Take it a step cuter with a hole punch to create an eyelet effect.

Supplies: Patterned paper (Collage Press); paper trim (Doodlebug); chipboard letter (Tim Holtz); buttons (Autumn Leaves, Making Memories); felt heart, paper flowers (Making Memories); hole punch (We R Memory Keepers); Misc: floss

How can I prevent my paper punches from crowding my space?

They're boxy. They're heavy. They're peculiar, not-quite-uniform shapes. It's hard to imagine punches being any clunkier or heavier. You might say it's hard to imagine organizing them without getting "punchy." They're definitely not the easiest tool to store—but many Masters have found that a little innovation goes a long way toward keeping them neatly organized and on hand.

⌃ Valerie Barton

Hey, punch junkies, check this out: Valerie Barton stores her punches in plastic drawers lined with paper to match her scrap room's décor—a basic idea you can totally take for your own. If you want to be extra organized, simply punch the shape onto a piece of cardstock or scrap paper, then adhere it to the front of the drawer or container the punch is stored in, as shown in the example above. This is a super easy way to know where all your punches are without having to actually look. Love it!

Photo by Holle WIktorek

︿ Holle Wiktorek

Holle Wiktorek is a true smarty-arty pants. She sorts her collection of circle, square and flower punches by shape and puts them on display in her scrap room inside wicker baskets labeled by shape. The open wicker baskets make it easy for her to grab a punch whenever she needs it. Less frequently used punches are stored in labeled decorative photo boxes. Holle is smart to separate her tools into those she uses often and those she doesn't.

Smooch

by Shannon Taylor

Now that you have those punches stored, don't let them collect dust! Breathe new life into flower paper punches by revealing only a portion of them. A pretty, modern border is the result.

Supplies: Cardstock; patterned paper (Scenic Route); letter stickers (American Crafts); brads (K&Co.); felt (Creative Imaginations); chipboard frame (Sandylion); ribbon (Wal-Mart); Misc: floss

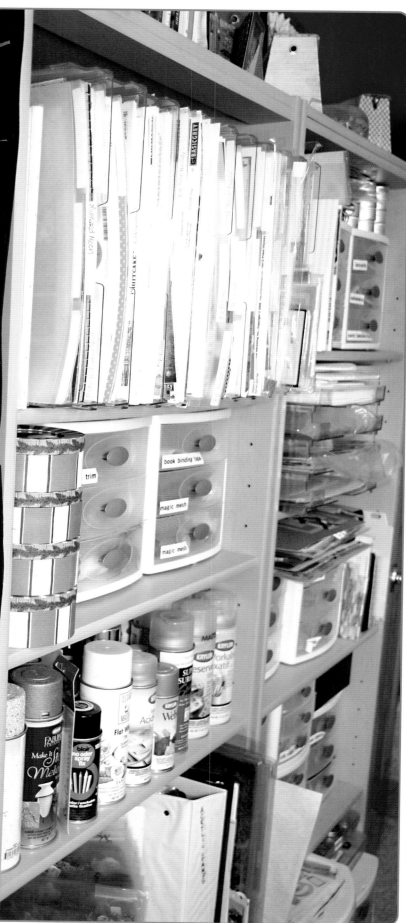

Photo by Christine Brown

? S.O.S! Stamps are a huge pain to organize—all those different shapes and sizes. Rescue me!

We love stamps because they are reusable. They make it look like we can draw or write in fancy letters. But we all experience S.O.S. (Stamp Overload Syndrome) from time to time. First, there are wood-mounted stamps. They are just bulky. Then, there are acrylic stamps. What they lack in bulk, they make up for in their ability to blend together. Finally, we have foam stamps. Hello, wrinkles and creases! Luckily the Masters have the answers to all these stamp-tastic riddles, whether you're looking to put your stash on display or you wish to hide it away.

« Christine Brown

Space exists everywhere. You just have to know how to find it. In the case of foam stamps, which can be tricky because they're easily damaged if not stored properly, Christine Brown came up with an especially creative option. She adhered Velcro to the backs of all of her foam stamps and attached them to fun foam sheets she hung on the side of one of her shelving units. They're organized in alphabetical order; all she has to do is walk up and select the one she needs of for her current project. "I love this system!" she says. "It takes up virtually no space and the stamps are always visible!"

The Whole Kitten Caboodle
by Christine Brown

With Christine's foam stamps so close at hand, making this layout was a snap. To get this effect, stamp the letters in acrylic paint onto a transparency. Cut out the shapes, adhere them to the chipboard circles and cover the whole thing with a dimensional glaze. Cute!

Supplies: Cardstock; patterned paper (Sweetwater); chipboard shapes (Bazzill); foam stamps (Li'l Davis, Making Memories); letter stickers (Creative Imaginations); brads (BoBunny); rhinestones (Heidi Swapp); die-cut phrase (Sweetwater); dimensional glaze (Ranger); Misc: Times New Roman font, circle cutter, ticket stubs

Photo by Suzy Plantamura

⌃ SuzyPlantamura

Suzy Plantamura's stamp collection is anything but vertically challenged. Suzy keeps her extensive wood-mounted stamp collection on a shelf above her workspace. Not only can she see them all at a glance, they also look pretty sweet lined up in a row. (FYI: Her alphabet stamps are tucked neatly in a box in her closet.)

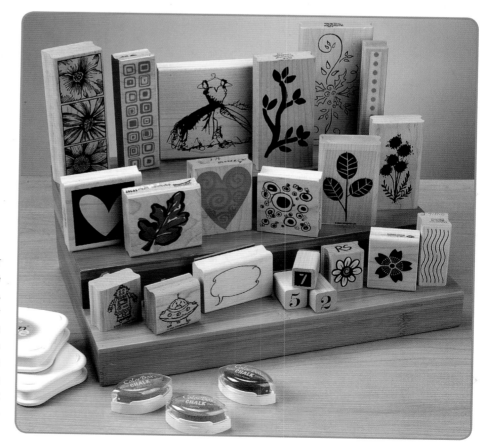

MasterSolution »

This just in: Spice racks are awesome for stamp storage! Whether they are of the rotating, desktop variety or wall-mounted, such as the one shown here, they get your stamps up and out of the drawer to where you can easily use them. Both Christine Brown and Iris Babao Uy have their own adaptations of this method, which keeps stamps where you can peep them without relying on purchasing any pricey shelves or organizers.

TracieRadtke »

If you share your scrap space with a communal area in your home, stamp storage can be awkward. Tracie Radtke keeps all her stamps in a big red decorative box that sits on top of her computer armoire. "I don't think people realize that it's a functional piece versus a decorative piece," she says.

Photo by Tracie Radtke

ExpertAdvice!
I may need a 12-step program for my Stamp Overload Syndrome. Do you have more ideas?

- Organize a popularity contest. Holle Wiktorek stores the stamps she uses most often in a container close to her workspace and stores the rest away to be retrieved only for the most involved projects.

- Get hip to a container no-brainer. Storage solutions come in all shapes, sizes and store aisles. Jessie Baldwin uses a container designed for nuts and bolts to store her stamps, and she never would have found it if she hadn't been wandering the hardware superstore. Lisa Tutman-Oglesby uses a two-tiered fruit basket to keep her stamp collection ripe and in season.

- Go for thrift-store chic. For a storage keep that's on the cheap, head to your local thrift stores or to the flea market. Jeniece Higgins and Shannon Taylor are two expert finders. Jeniece uses an old printer's block shelf to store her stamps in the uncommonly slim drawers. Shannon uses a vintage suitcase to store her wood-mounted stamps. It's decorative (she embellished hers with the words "my getting pretty box") *and* portable.

- Hello, acrylic. These stamps take up much less space in storage and can be organized in clever ways. Many Masters store them in the plastic-sleeve pages of a three-ring binder, which are easy to flip through. Iris Babao Uy stores them in CD jewel cases small enough to keep right on her desktop.

Warm Holiday Memories
by Susan Cyrus

The acrylic stamps Susan used in this layout are stored in old DVD cases. Susan says, "I coat the backs with Aleene's Tack It Over & Over and that allows me to adhere them to the acrylic block and then again to the DVD case when not in use."

Supplies: Cardstock; unmounted stamps (Ma Vinci); sticker accents (Making Memories); Misc: Dearest Swash font, ink

? I am endlessly amazed and befuddled by the variety of necessary scrapbooking adhesives. How does one organize them all?

There was once a time when a scrapbooker needed just one, maybe two, types of adhesive. But as many scrapbookers blossom into closet mixed-media artists, an arsenal of adhesives is a necessity. You will need to take care in organizing your adhesives as they can be leaky, messy, bulky and generally yucky to look at. It's a good idea to keep them self-contained and away from heat and sunlight.

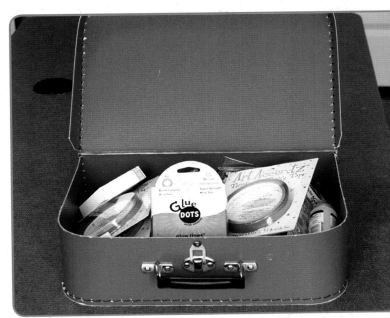

Photo by Greta Hammond

GretaHammond »

Greta Hammond is a bit of an adhesive junkie. "I buy multiple quantities of adhesive when it goes on sale so that I always have some handy!" Her open adhesives sit conveniently in her desk drawer while the overstock gets the top treatment in the decorative suitcase shown here.

« MasterSoution

As a scrapbooker, you will always need glue, so adhesives are the perfect supply to keep tucked away in a drawer. You won't run the risk of outta sight, outta mind, and the drawer will hide the ugly ducklings that tend to leak. You can use one big dresser drawer, like Catherine Feegel-Erhardt does, or you can group adhesives by task and divide them into smaller drawers. Those who like it to be portable should opt for multidrawer craft carts. "I have an adhesive cart," Samantha Walker says. "Did I just say that out loud? I have a cart that houses mostly adhesives of various kinds. It's crazy that I would have that much adhesive."

HolleWiktorek »

Storage solutions for adhesive can be pretty, too, as Holle Wiktorek demonstrates. She adds some decorative spice by storing it in wicker baskets lined with decorative fabric. The fabric will protect your shelf, desktop or floor from any minor leaks or drips. Simply sort and label by type: liquid, foam, tape, etc.

Photo by Holle Wiktorek

Chapter Three | Materials

Strange, isn't it, how scrapbooking materials seem to misbehave once they are brought home from the store? In the store, they act like good little brads and eyelets and buttons and ribbons, quiet and tidy in their shiny packaging. Once home, they become birds of a different feather, scattering around, mingling with each other and, sometimes, getting into tangles. Baaad little products!

It's high time to show these products who's boss. Truthfully, the only place where these materials should be allowed to play with reckless abandon is on your layouts. In order for that to happen, you, boss, will need to have some discipline of your own. On the following pages, the Masters dish their most divine secrets for keeping the scrap stations and rooms under control. No more embellishments duking it out, competing for space in your desk drawers or overflowing bins. Soon your stickers and rub-ons will be living in orderly, neighborly harmony next to your eyelets and flowers, and all will be right with the world.

My paper is seriously out of control—how can I give it a little more grace?

At the core of every scrapbooker, there lies an obsession with patterned paper—some just hide it better than others! But really, where would any of us be without our paper stashes? It's the fundamental component for scrapbooking—even more important than the scrapbook itself. If paper is your most abundant supply (for some of us, paper outnumbers all of our other supplies combined), it stands to reason that it poses the biggest threat to your organizational harmony. Whether you're looking for a storage method that's over the top or under the radar, the Masters have got you covered.

Photo by Heidi Schueller

⌃ **Heidi**Schueller

No, the photo above was not taken in a scrapbooking store, but that's what Heidi Schueller's kids always tell her it reminds them of! In her self-described "very small but perfect" 6' × 10' (183cm × 305cm) basement studio, Heidi's husband constructed this amazing wooden paper rack right on the wall to store her giant supply of unused sheets. "I am surrounded by paper! I love paper, and it's my biggest supply." She sorts it according to color and by company. Paper scraps are later relegated to a tall plastic bin or a three-drawer plastic organizer, depending on their size. And, of course, they're also sorted by color.

StaciEtheridge »

If your husband isn't quite as motivated as Heidi's or you don't have the space, check out Staci Etheridge's penchant for patterned paper storage. "I found these great plastic scrapfolios that have handles and dividers. I bought enough to sort my paper by ROYGBIV and a few extras. The folios then line up in huge galvanized bins that slide in and out of my desk cabinet." There's room for cardstock there, too.

Photo by Staci Etheridge

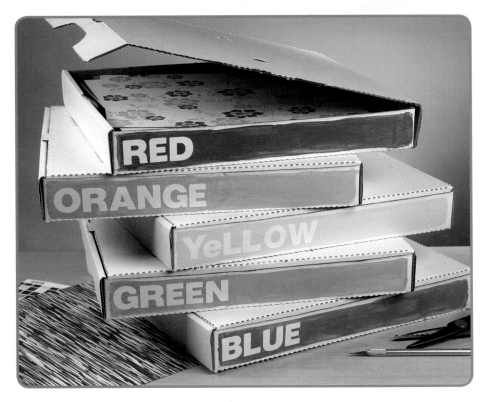

« **Angelia**Wigginton

Angelia Wigginton's advice for storing paper makes us hungry! On family pizza night, Angelina requests a few extra (clean) pizza boxes, which she uses to store her scrap paper (they work great for finished layouts, too!). Simply decorate them so you know what's inside. For a variation on this method, try Caroline Ikeji's approach: She recycles used Priority Mail boxes instead. She slices the boxes in half diagonally, sits them upright and stores her paper in them vertically (also a great way to store other sheets of embellishments, or even inspirational magazines).

Crystal Jeffrey Rieger »

Even the most organized scrap-paper stash looks a tad unruly. Keeping it contained is the best anyone can hope for. Crystal Jeffrey Rieger stores her scrap paper in a three-drawer unit. Each drawer is dedicated to a color temperature: warm, cool and neutral. Whenever she has leftover pieces at her craft table, she simply sorts them by their color family and *voilà!* It's worth noting that this approach is in contrast to her method of storing patterned paper: Paper from her favorite manufacturers is stored by company and the rest is all together on a separate shelf. "I just shuffle through it until I find something I need," she says. "I cannot organize papers by color type or pattern. I find it very limiting, and I know I would never maintain it."

Photo by Crystal Jeffrey Rieger

The Dark Side of the Force
by Crystal Jeffrey Rieger

Now that your cardstock is so easy to access, take a stab at customizing your own cardstock shapes. Crystal created this shape and cut it out for her background. So easy!

Supplies: Cardstock (Worldwin); letter stickers, rub-on letters (American Crafts); acrylic stars (Heidi Swapp); doodle template (Crafter's Workshop); Misc: hole punch

Susan Weinroth »

Paper cuts suck, so Susan Weinroth stores all her paper scraps in hanging files separated by color, which makes for easy and safe sorting. The Cropper Hopper vertical storage units work perfectly with hanging files as well. This method is a great choice for those who crop on the go, as the folders are an easy grab when packing for a crop.

Photo by Susan Weinroth

ExpertAdvice!

What are some other ways to hide, er, solve my paper problems?

- Embrace your bad habits. "My biggest mess maker is paper," says Tracy Austin. "I like to make page kits and I tend to pull waaaay more paper than I need. Of course, I never return those extra sheets to their home. So for those stray sheets, I store them in a file folder for miscellaneous papers and turn there first for paper selection for my next project. Instead of fighting my laziness, I embrace it. It helps keep the snowball of mess from starting in the first place."

- Wheel in. Wheel out. If your living space doubles as your scrap space, Hillary Heidelberg recommends keeping papers on a rolling cart. She rolls her paper cart into her scrap area when she is working and rolls it out when she is finished.

- Safety first. Know the weakness of your storage system. Jodi Heinen, for example, stores paper in wire racks, but knows that this can bend the corners of the sheets on the bottom of each one. So she simply lines the racks with cardboard.

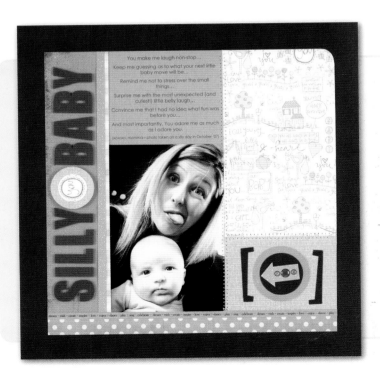

Silly Baby
by Susan Weinroth

Susan's hanging file folder system for storing paper scraps makes it easy for her to find patterned papers that coordinate. For a cohesive look with a variety of papers, try creating custom embellishments from the paper, like Susan did for the circle accents on this layout.

Supplies: Cardstock; patterned paper (BasicGrey, Heidi Grace, KI Memories, Sassafras Lass); letter stickers (American Crafts); rub-on trim (Heidi Grace); acrylic dots (Cloud 9); paper punches (Fiskars); Misc: Century Gothic font, thread

My lettering accents are only slightly more organized than alphabet soup. Spell out a solution for me.

It all starts innocently enough. You purchase a few packs of chipboard ABC's, and you purchase a few more. You start to use said packs of ABC's and suddenly, you've got more X's and O's than any respectable person can handle. If you're not minding your organizational P's and Q's, making sense of it all could be more frustrating than the last round of a Scrabble match. Luckily, these solutions are as easy as A, B, C. (We'd say no pun intended, but who are we kidding?)

⌃ MasterSoution

Want to make straggler letters a nonissue? Use this tried-and-true, Master-approved method. Just find a container that has 26 small compartments, give or take, and use it to organize your individual letters. Label the compartments and off you go. Not finding what you need in the home organization department? Try the hardware store. The organizer shown here was designed to hold nuts and bolts. You can find everything right when you need it, and you won't need a wheel of fortune to tell you that you have to buy a vowel.

Samantha Walker »

Organizing letter and rub-on stickers can be a bit more of a task. But task Master Samantha Walker keeps it simple by sorting them into protective plastic sleeves clipped into a three-ring binder (the cover of which is decorated with, you guessed it, even more letters [see below!]). It's literally letter perfect with options for every layout.

Photos by Samantha Walker

Photo by Michele Skinner

≪ MicheleSkinner

Since her scrap space is in a communal area, a fairly large storage unit with drawers for every chipboard letter isn't quite feasible for Michele Skinner. Her solution? Envelopes labeled with letter stickers and tucked alphabetically into a bin.

ExpertAdvice!

What are other tips for storing chipboard letters?

- Consider the size. Christine Brown sorts her letters by size—that way she knows where to go for a layout that calls for a monogram or one that calls for a more subtle lettering.
- Consider the use. Tracy Austin points out that some letters are interchangeable in many of the font alphabets. For this reason, she stores lowercase B's and Q's together, D's and P's together and U's and N's together whenever possible.
- Consider the source. Tracy Austin also stores her letters by manufacturer, sorted into jewelry organizers. Some other Masters store "naked" chipboard separate from patterned or colored letters.
- Consider the course. Alternative storage solutions are virtually limitless. For example, Katrina Simeck sorts her chipboard letters and other embellishments into a hanging shoe organizer that hangs flat on the wall or in a closet. The pockets are perfectly sized and can be labeled easily.

Xmas Stuff

by Michele Skinner

With all of her chipboard separated by letter group, it was easy for Michele to lay out all the X's and find the perfect one to divide this 12" × 12" (30cm × 30cm) page. Look at your letters with an eye toward their design possibilities as well as to what they can spell.

Supplies: Cardstock; patterned paper (Daisy D's, Scrapworks); chipboard letter (Zsiage); letter stickers (K&Co.); rub-on letters (American Crafts); brads (Doodlebug, Karen Foster); Misc: Wendy Medium font, string

I need a less disastrous way to store my rub-ons. Whatcha got?

Sure, we all love rub-ons. They are easy-peasy to use and leave such a clean, finished look. But once you start to cut the sheets apart to use them, they get this kind of disheveled look about them. Backing sheets become separated, tools for rubbing become lost, and it becomes harder and harder to find what you need. Interestingly enough, you probably already have everything you need on hand to best organize these clever materials!

Katrina Simeck »

Organize your rub-ons by theme. They come in so many, it just makes the most sense. To keep them tidy, Katrina Simeck suggests keeping categories together by punching a hole in the top left corner of each sheet and threading them all onto a binder ring or oversized jump ring. Then you can clip them into a binder, hang them from a pegboard or bulletin board, or store them in a box. How easy is that?

« Brittany Laakkonen

Rub-on. Rub-off. It's a simple concept, but once the backing sheet becomes separated from the rub-on sheet, as it often does, scrapbookers become unglued. To keep the rub-on from rubbing off on other surfaces (a true waste of a favorite supply), Brittany Laakkonen simply staples the backing sheet to each page of rub-ons before storing them in a box in her basement scrap space (a sanctuary in a house filled by her family of nine). This method makes her rub-on collection that much easier to quickly grab and spread out on her favorite place to scrap: the floor.

Photo by Nic Howard

⌃ NicHoward

To call Nic Howard's scrap space a room is using the term loosely. The 8' × 8' (244cm × 244cm) box—barely bigger than a closet—has been affectionately nicknamed "the bat cave" by her hubby. (Still, what some of us wouldn't give for a bat cave of our own!) At least rub-ons are tiny, so there's always room for them. Lone rub-ons get sorted with stickers into small, flat plastic containers labeled by theme and stored on a higher shelf. Packets, though, get a luxury home in a contemporary wicker basket on a shelf just above her workspace. Simple, accessible and pretty to look at.

Enjoy Everyday
by Greta Hammond

Who would have thought that a simple rub-on could do so much to unify a layout? Here the swirly green rub-on crosses the two contrasting patterned papers and reaches all the way up to the photo in the corner, tying all the elements together in spectacular fashion.

Supplies: Brads, fabric tape, patterned paper, stickers (Déjà Views); Misc: Batik Regular font

I'm not very sticker savvy. How can I get them organized?

Talk about sticker shock. Sitting down to organize stacks of stickers is nobody's dream of a Sunday afternoon, but it can be fun. Pawing through all of your stickers can make you feel like a kid again, only this time, your sticker collection totally takes the cake. When organizing them, figure out a way that best works for you. This could be hanging file folders, a binder or simply a basket. Read on for some suggestions worth sticking with.

⌃ SamanthaWalker

For you Type A organizers, take a tip from Samantha Walker and store them in a binder with plastic sleeves, complete with labeled tabs, to make it even easier for you to find what you're looking for. This way you can page through your collection without the fear of getting into a sticky sticker situation.

« MasterSolution

You could store your stickers by color, but you'd be hating yourself in no time. Stickers should be stored by theme. Case closed. If your collection is especially large, Tracie Radtke recommends keeping your favorites in clear view so you remember to use them. Suzy Plantamura adds that kids love stickers, so if these fun supplies are readily available, your little ones will be more apt to get creative with you. If you decide to use a basket or bin, as shown here, Crystal Jeffrey Rieger recommends lining them up by size so you can see at least a little bit of every sheet in your stash—a tiered magazine rack is a perfect way to store stickers in this manner.

I do laundry, so I know I can fold—how can I transfer this skill set to fabric and felt?

The Masters feel you on fabric and felt. These softies are great to have on hand, but they require maintenance and can be tricky to store. If anything spills on them, they could be ruined. If anything catches on a piece, it could be snagged or ripped, and if it gets wrinkled, you may have to—ew—iron. Being smart about storing your fabric and felt ensures your scrap time will be more fun than work.

Photo by Susan Weinroth

⌃ Susan Weinroth

A room without a closet. Is there anything worse? Probably. But Susan Weinroth has such a room, so it motivates her to find attractive storage solutions that can sit out in the open on shelves. This basket of folded quarter blocks of fabric, sorted by colors of the rainbow, is a perfect example of her ideal approach.

SusanWeinroth »

Continuing bravely on her closet-less organizational quest, Susan Weinroth keeps larger pieces of solid-colored fabric carefully folded in another basket and leftover scraps of fabric in colorful pails where she can clearly see what she has left.

Photo by Susan Weinroth

Home

by Susan Weinroth

Fabric is the perfect medium to use in this cozy layout about the comforts of home. If you find yourself with a growing stash of fabric (and that's easy to do), consider purchasing a separate set of scissors and shears just for cutting fabric (and avoid dulling them by using them to cut paper).

Supplies: Cardstock; fabric; brads, chipboard hearts, metal stickers, photo turn (Heidi Grace); stamps (Fiskars, Hero Arts); pinking shears, scallop shears (Fiskars); Misc: buttons, thread

Have a nice day, I guess.

Photo by Staci Etheridge

« StaciEtheridge

Staci Etheridge punches a hole in the top corner of each piece of felt or fabric in her stash and then strings them all on a loop, using a circle of ribbon or a binder ring. This approach—reminiscent of fabric swatches on display at a furniture store—is handy both for storage and for transportation. And it keeps fabric safe from damage or wrinkles.

CrystalJeffreyRieger »

Crystal Jeffrey Rieger's approach to felt gives us the warm fuzzies. She keeps felt squares rolled up, rather than folded, to prevent wrinkling or creasing. She stands them up in two flowerpots on her tabletop for a touch of color. Her sewing machine stays at the other end of the table, ready when inspiration strikes. She has a set approach to her organization. "I found what works best for me: open containers so I can see my supplies but within that container everything can just be tossed in."

Photo by Crystal Jeffrey Rieger

Reluctant Rider

by Amy Peterman

While the felt bracket Amy uses here is actually die-cut, you can create the same type of embellishment from your felt or fabric stash. Simply freehand cut the design, or trace a template onto the back of the felt and cut it out with scissors.

Supplies: Cardstock; patterned paper (American Crafts, Sandylion); brad, letters, stamp (Autumn Leaves); rub-ons (7gypsies, KI Memories); sticker accents (7gypsies, Sandylion); decorative tape (7gypsies); felt (Fancy Pants); ribbon (Scrapworks); Misc: decorative scissors, ink, paint

Do they make a detangler solution for fibers and threads? Mine are in need of a deep condition.

You're in the heat of creating an amazing layout, and it dawns on you that it needs a little something, a little . . . FIBER! But, wait, the creativity is stalled by a giant rat's nest of knots and strands. This is no way to create! Especially if the knots are so bad you have to get out the scissors. Keeping your fibers and threads lovely and organized could be one of the biggest time-savers you're not taking advantage of. And, it's easier than you think with these clever solutions from some Masters who are true fiber fans.

« LisaTutman-Oglesby

When one of her favorite local scrapbook stores closed, Lisa Tutman-Oglesby made the best of a bad situation and purchased some of the displays that had been in use there. Among them were four-sided swivels with pegboards that lent themselves perfectly to organizing and storing ribbons and fibers. Once she got started with this method—and filled them all up quickly—she loved it so much that she wanted to create a similar unit on her own to store her massive collection of thread in every imaginable color. The result? This easy-to-make rack—a thread aficionado's dream. To make your own, simply visit your local craft store and purchase some individual thread racks. Then buy a large, unfinished wooden board and use wood screws to attach all of the thread racks, lining them up vertically on the board and attaching them foot-to-foot for a seamless look. Decorate the board however you'd like, and hang it on the wall or prop it up for an easily accessible display.

Photo by Lisa Tutman-Oglesby

IrisBabaoUy »

Iris Babao Uy wins the ingenuity award when it comes to organizing, and this is one of her favorite creations. These spice jars have tiny holes in the tops that are just big enough to thread the strands of fibers through. "When I need a certain fiber, I just pull it from the container, cut it and I'm done! It's never messy, and I see all of my fibers at one glance." Best of all, she can always see how much she has left—no over-estimating that there's more wound around a spool than there really is and running out halfway through a project.

Photo by Iris Babao Uy

Bliss
by Amelia McIvor

Amelia created this fiber fabulous layout using a few basic tools, some embroidery floss and a good bit of patience. Draw your design onto cardstock, then punch the sewing holes wth a paper piercer to make the sewing go more quickly.

Supplies: Cardstock; patterned paper (American Crafts, Urban Lily); hole punch, paper piercer (Making Memories); rub-on letters (Heidi Grace); Misc: Architect and Harting fonts, decorative scissors, floss

My pretty ribbon just doesn't deserve the mess it's in. How can I treat it better?

Ribbon is a fluid supply. You can fold it, bend it, wrap it, hang it, tie it and loop it, and the storage solutions that follow capitalize on this trait. Ribbon is as easy to organize as it is fun and pretty to organize. It's a natural choice for adding a decorative touch to your organizational system. If only everything in life were tied up all neat and tidy in a big bow.

⌃ AmeliaMcIvor

Until ribbon manufacturers create better packaging, scrapbookers will need to explore creative ways to organize it. Anyone who's gone on a wrapping spree during the holiday season knows what we're talking about. That's why Amelia McIvor simply discards the packaging entirely and instead wraps her ribbons around index cards or playing cards for easy storage—grouped by color—in a simple shoe box. This is especially handy since she doesn't have a designated scrap space—she just grabs what she needs and settles in at the dining room table.

AmyPeterman »

For Amy Peterman, the Clip-It-Up free-standing, rotating organizer is the ultimate ribbon storage solution. She's devoted the entire top tier to her collection. She simply wraps her ribbon onto chipboard cards, then hangs them from the swivel clips. Selecting the right ribbon for a project is as simple as a quick spin.

Photo by Amy Peterman

Little Stink Bug
by Shannon Taylor

While Shannon loves her ribbon storage solution (turn to page 82 to see it in action), she loves using her ribbon stash even more. For this look, cover premade metal letters with ribbon, one strip at a time, and trim to the shape of the letters.

Supplies: Cardstock; metal letters, white letter stickers (American Crafts); ribbon (Making Memories, Wal-Mart); transparency overlay (Hambly); bug clip art by Jessica Edwards (Designer Digitals); Misc: Marketing Script font, bubble wrap

Caroline Ikeji »

Spooled ribbon makes it easy to slip, slide and take your ribbon away to the land of neat and tidy. Caroline Ikeji stores her spools of ribbon on hangers. She simply breaks the bottom rung of the hanger and slides them on (hint: hangers of a sturdier variety are your best bet). And since she scraps in her bedroom, this storage solution helps make the most of her space. If your collection is small, a hook hanging over the door or from a drawer should do the trick. If your collection is large, the options are only as limited as your spare closet space!

Photo by Shannon Taylor

« Shannon Taylor

Organizational items are lurking everywhere—you just have to look for them. They can be in the garage, in the basement, in your neighbor's garage (make sure they are having a garage sale before you start rummaging through their stuff, though). Shannon Taylor has several vintage finds (including an antique bookcase) in her dedicated scrap room just off her kitchen, but her storage solution for ribbon is her favorite. "I purchased this item for $2 at a yard sale in my neighborhood. It's a wood display that hangs on the wall and is supposed to be used to display a matchbook collection. Instead, I have a bundle of color on my wall! It's so easy to see what I want and just pull the ribbons off. Plus I can carry my layout over to the display and hold it up to compare colors. *Love it!*"

⌃ **Katrina**Simeck

It's amazing ribbon causes such a fuss when it comes to organizing. It's ribbon, for goodness sake; it will wrap around anything. Katrina Simeck wraps hers on old-fashioned clothespins and clips the ends so they won't unravel. For a more contemporary or space-saving approach, you can opt for bulldog clips instead.

ExpertAdvice!

What are some solutions for smaller collections or for ribbon scraps?

- Zip it up. Staci Etheridge sorts her ribbon by color into small plastic bags that zip securely closed to prevent tangling.

- Hang it up. Sheila Doherty hangs her ribbon spools from a pegboard. She ties loose strands onto binder rings and hangs them from the pegboard, too.

- Hide it away. Hillary Heidelberg rarely uses her ribbon, so she stores it under her bed to save more accessible space for regularly used materials.

- Recycle. Valerie Barton uses leftover ribbon scraps to label containers for other supplies that are organized by color. For example, her paper folders are labeled with pieces of ribbon that match the colors of the paper stored inside.

The brads and eyelets are conspiring against me. So many! So tiny! Help!

Conventionally, brads and eyelets are stored in tiny containers. They come from the store that way so it seems to make sense to store them like that. That's fine and dandy, but there are other, more creative ways to store your eyelets and brads. Leave it to the Masters to figure it out.

⌃ **Master**Solution

"Honey, have you seen my tackle box?" Many of the Masters have heard this question from their husbands after they swiped the compartmentalized containers for their stash of brads and eyelets. If your husband is no fisherman, you can purchase a brand-new tackle box (they are ridiculously cheap) or purchase a shiny new compartmentalized container, available in the home organization section of many stores. Sort by color, color family or favorite color combos so you can find what you need when you need it without having to get out a million small containers or root through one big one.

AmyPeterman »

Never underestimate the potential of a bulletin board. Amy Peterman figured if it's good enough for tacks, it's good enough for brads. She simply sticks the pointed sides of brads into the cork, grouping colors together in a rainbow (an idea she got from scrapinstyletv.com). They are easy to remove and add cheer and charm to her scrap room.

Photo by Amy Peterman

ExpertAdvice!
Gimme, gimme more ideas for storing brads and eyelets!

- Think boxy, foxy. Catherine Feegel-Erhardt stores hers in old cigar boxes for a vintage look.

- Spice is nice. Lisa Tutman-Oglesby suggests using a rotating spice rack as an easy and affordable way to store brads and eyelets of all kinds. Holle Wiktorek also recycles spice jars by using them to store her brads.

- Be a magnito bandito. Kelly Goree stores her brads and eyelets in metal tins that she then attaches magnets to and sticks to the side of a metal storage cabinet.

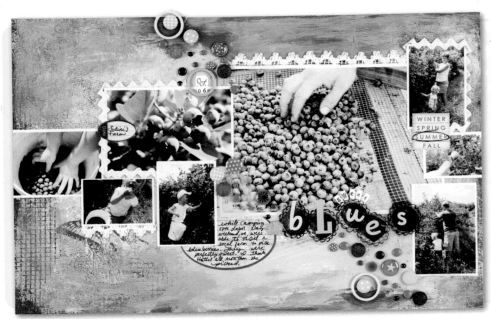

Sweet Blues
by Amy Peterman

With her brads organized on the cork-board, finding just the right ones to use in this layout couldn't have been easier. If you find that the tones of your photos don't quite match your patterned paper, try adding a bit of paint to tie it all together, as Amy did here.

Supplies: Patterned paper (Lazar); brads (Autumn Leaves, K&Co., Making Memories, Paper Studio, Queen & Co., Scrapworks); letter stickers, sticker accents (EK Success, Making Memories, Melissa Frances, SEI); stamps (Autumn Leaves); trims (Offray); Misc: ink, paint

And what about beads and buttons?

Beads and buttons, like brads and eyelets, are tiny supplies that can make a mighty mess of your studio space. Also like brads and eyelets, you can find decorative ways to store and display them. In fact, because of their variety, uniform shapes and rainbow of colors, beads and buttons look awesome in bowls, jars and other clear containers. Displaying them is a great way to add color to your space.

LisaPace »

In the right container, beads and buttons can be kind of knick-knacky. Lisa Pace makes use of old-fashioned glass candy jars to store her extensive collection of beads and buttons. She organizes them by season—bright colors together for summer, rich colors together for fall, etc. The clear glass allows her to see her entire selection at a glance, and the tight lids prevent spills if they're knocked over. Plus, they look almost good enough to eat.

« MasterSolution

Bumbling for buttons and beads can take serious time away from scrapbooking. Most Masters agree sorting is an absolute must. To get the job done, compartmentalized containers are a popular choice. Choose one with fewer and larger compartments than the tackle box you're eyeing for your brads. Kathy Fesmire sorts her buttons and beads by warm, cool and neutral colors. Katrina Simeck opts for bud vases—they're just right if you like to pour the selection of buttons out in front of you and comb through them to find the perfect one.

Photo by Lisa Pace

Fancy Express
by Heidi Schueller

Beads plus buttons equals fabulous homemade embellishments. To re-create this look, apply crystal lacquer to the top of clear buttons, then sprinkle on seed beads and let dry. Heidi added a few beads to the centers of the paper flowers as well, to continue the theme throughout the page.

Supplies: Patterned paper (Cosmo Cricket, Crate Paper, My Mind's Eye); stamps (Lazar, Stampabilities); beads (Darice, Queen & Co.); flowers (Bazzill, Prima); rub-on (Frances Meyer); journaling paper (Imagination Project); swirl template (Crafter's Workshop); crystal lacquer (Sakura); Misc: buttons, ink, ribbon, thread

How can I keep my flower embellishments looking as fresh as a farm daisy?

You could wrap them in tissue paper and store them safely in their own drawer, but what fun would that be? Flowers are beautiful and meant to be seen and, you know, arranged. You just have to decide how. You can use your flowers to create adorable bouquets throughout your studio or workspace. Just take care to protect them from dust.

⌃ MasterSolution

Imagine, your very own scrapbooking greenhouse. It's full of flowers that invite spring inside and chase away the winter blahs. As with other small and plentiful embellishments, most Masters store their flowers by color—and they're so pretty that clear glass bottles are a popular choice. But there's no need to go out and buy fancy new containers: Valerie Barton, for example, cleverly uses leftover Starbucks Frappucino bottles to store her blooms.

Tracy Austin »

Tracy Austin's basket full of flowers looks as if she picked them herself. Here, they all have room to breathe. If you like to take them with you to crops or want to protect them from dust or curious pets or children, simply purchase one with a lid that closes when you need it to, or drape the basket with a beautiful piece of scrap fabric.

Photo by Tracy Austin

Girl Child

by Tracy Austin

Using paint, buttons and those blooms from her basket, Tracy created a clever color-block design for this layout. And cleanup couldn't have been easier; all the blooms she decided not to use here were tossed back into the basket.

Supplies: Cardstock; patterned paper (Paper Studio); chipboard letters (Heidi Swapp); letter stickers (American Crafts); flowers (Prima); buttons (Autumn Leaves); Misc: floss, paint

? I need to make my bling sing. How do I organize rhinestones and sequins?

The glitz, the glitter, the sparkly. No one blames you for being a glamour hound, but when it threatens to take over your scrap space, you need an intervention, sister. It seems like there's an unspoken rule that the smaller the embellishment, the more you have of it, which means the more important it is to keep it sorted. Keeping tiny embellishments like rhinestones and sequins in their original packaging is just not practical—they end up taking up much more room than they need to, and spills are almost inevitable. But once you pour them out, it's fairly easy to find an efficient system that works for you.

⌃ MasterSolution

Nine out of ten Memory Makers Masters agree: When in doubt, compartmentalize! Rhinestones and sequins lend themselves to this old standby of organizational methods. Whether you choose a tray that doubles as a pretty decoration (Nicole Stark admits she's one of those "If I don't see it, I won't use it" scrappers), or a box with a tight-fitting lid for easy transportation (Jessie Baldwin favors an old-fashioned tackle box), sorting by color and/or size makes this method undeniably functional.

⌃ **Heidi**Schueller

Heidi Schueller is fond of using empty, washed-out medicine bottles to store her smallest embellishments. You can label them, pour them out to sort through your stash, grab them for cropping on the go, you name it. Best of all, recycling is good for the planet—and for your scrapbooking budget.

Sister Love

by Suzy Plantamura

With two daughters and a personal love of bling, Suzy has all kinds of storage solutions for her rhinestones. Try keeping loose rhinestones in a container right at your desk, so that they're within reach when inspiration strikes.

Supplies: Cardstock; patterned paper (BoBunny); chipboard letters (K&Co.); rhinestone circles and word (Me & My Big Ideas); Misc: ink.

When it comes to ink, I'm hardly tickled pink. I need better ways to store them, please tell me what you think.

Welcome to the Masters' ThINK Tank. This is the place where they solve your problems of dried-up ink pads and teach you how to properly store them for the greatest longevity. Tip: When storing pads and embossing powders, the most important thing is making sure they're tightly sealed. Beyond that, simply choose the method most compatible with the size of your stash and the space you have available.

Master Solution

Inks have a tendency to dry out over time. To keep them "juicy," many manufacturers—and Masters—recommend storing them upside down in a plastic drawer. Many manufacturers note the color of the ink on the bottom, making it easy to find the one you're looking for—but if it's not noted (or if you need a magnifying glass to read it), it's easy to make your own label with a color swatch and/or the name.

IrisBabaoUy »

Iris Babao Uy had the clever idea of storing her embossing powders on this cute flatware organizer turned on its side to create shelves. Powders are organized by use and are readily accessible.

Photo by Iris Babao Uy

Enjoy

by Lisa Tutman-Oglesby

With all that juicy ink handy, you'll want to stamp it on every layout! To create dimensional stamped embellishments, stamp each design twice, cut each one out and layer them using staples or glue.

Supplies: Cardstock; rubber stamps (Autumn Leaves, Fancy Pants, Heidi Swapp, Rubber Café); flower (Prima); chipboard accents (Trace Industries); number stickers (EK Success); paper trim, tab (My Mind's Eye); brads (Hot Off The Press); Misc: floss, paint, transparency

? My language can get pretty colorful when dealing with my paints and paintbrushes. Can you help me clean it up?

Paints and paintbrushes are wonderful artist tools but can be a total pain in the behind. Scrapbookers who enjoy the look of painting on their layouts fall in one of two categories: those who think making a mess is fun and those who find messy tools and techniques kind of stressful. Regardless of whether or not they find fun in mess making, everyone hates cleaning it up. Organizing your messy supplies will make making a mess a cleaner endeavor. You'll have fewer spills to worry about and errant paintbrushes to chase after.

HeidiSchueller »

Heidi Schueller's husband came to her rescue again (we love him!). She found black round metal baskets at a local office supply store and asked her handy hubby to cut appropriately sized circles into her countertop work surface to hold them all. What a perfect way to keep these paint-brushes (as well as liquid-filled paint markers and other pens) upright, organized and within easy reach.

Photo by Heidi Schueller

«**Catherine** Feegel-**Erhardt**

Painting with foam brushes is awesome because it's so easy, and they are so easy to clean, but what happens when you're right in the middle of a project and the phone rings, duty calls or your public awaits? The darn things dry out! Catherine Feegel-Erhardt's practical troubleshooting method is to house them in plastic bags that zip closed. That way, the bags are always on hand when you take them out to work. You can simply return them to the bags to keep them from drying out in the middle of a project. Better yet, the bags double as a way to protect your work surface from the mess, too. Afterward, wash both the bag and the brush before storing them away.

Photo by Lisa Pace

LisaPace »

If paint were money, Lisa Pace would be rich! She keeps those she uses most often near her scrap desk in a wire star container she received as a gift. She loves it because it is both cute and functional.

Dishes Smishes

by Samantha Walker

The truth of the matter is that paintbrushes do start to show their age. When that's the case, try a tiered method of storing them, like Samantha does. Her very best brushes, used for fine detail work on the lettering and accent spots on this layout, are stored carefully with a plastic tube around the bristles. Her old brushes, with stiff bristles that work well for grungier painting as on the word tags here, are in an open container at her desk, unprotected but at the ready.

Supplies: Cardstock; patterned paper (Chatterbox); ribbon (Chatterbox, Offray); ribbon slides (Making Memories); paints (Plaid)

Photo by Lisa Pace

« LisaPace

So many paints, so little time. Poor Lisa Pace (or lucky Lisa Pace, depending on your point of view) has so many paints that, in addition to her decorative wire star (shown on page 95), she must also employ a practical approach for storing the rest of her supply. She keeps all her paints sorted by color family in a clear pocket shoe organizer hanging on the inside of the closet door in her scrap room. The clear vinyl makes it easy to see all the paints at a glance and to rinse out or wipe up any leaks. Each pocket allows plenty of room for multiple bottles.

GretaHammond »

If vertical paint storage is not your idea of a pretty picture, you might prefer Greta Hammond's solution. She keeps her paints sorted in two narrow linen boxes. This allows the bottles to stand up straight to avoid leakage or spilling, and she can easily pull out the boxes and look for whatever color she needs at the moment. Lids make them easy to transport if and when the need to crop on the run arises.

Photo by Greta Hammond

ExpertAdvice!
Can you paint me a picture of some other ways to store this favorite supply?

• Be proactive. Samantha Walker, mommy of three, is a true master at preventing messes before they start. "I just move my project to the kitchen when I need to do some painting on it," she says. "I actually keep my paintbrushes in the kitchen so I can be by the sink when I want to rinse them."

• Share and share alike. Valerie Barton knows her kids like to use her paints, so she keeps them in a hall closet in a portable container so the kids don't "mess up" her scrap space looking for them.

• Go your own way. Diana Graham stores paints in a spinning spice rack. Jessie Baldwin keeps all supplies related to painting in one container. Staci Etheridge opts for a decorative suitcase. Do whatever works for you.

Chapter Four | Digital Supplies

If you think the digital era cuts down on your supplies, think again. While digital resources minimize the physical space necessary to house more traditional scrapbooking supplies, they still require diligent organization attention. They won't litter your desk, but they'll do worse: They'll litter your computer. And especially if you use your computer for work, that's a mix of business and pleasure you will want to live without.

So, what's there to organize? Well, there are the gazillion digital photos you take and leave on memory cards, flash drives, your computer desktop and hard drive. There are hard backups of those images on disks. Digital software, kits, FONTS! Oh, and let's not forget finished digital layouts, right? All of this will add up quickly if you don't nip it in the bud. Thankfully, this chapter will motivate you to harmonize your digital realm. Who better than the Masters to help you organize your virtual scrapbook station? Turn the page to get organized digitally, both on screen and in your scrap space.

Holy digital photo files!
How do I organize all these images?

If anything is going to save you time and make you more productive, it's naming and organizing your digital image files. Seriously. It's time to stop the denial, stop the rationalizations, stop the madness. When you upload those images, take a few minutes to create some folders and name tags, and for the love of humanity, use dates! Then, once you've uploaded them, clean off that memory card so it's ready for the next round. Oh yeah, and make backups. If that hard drive crashes, you won't give two thoughts to IRS files and home budgets, but you will *sob* over lost photos.

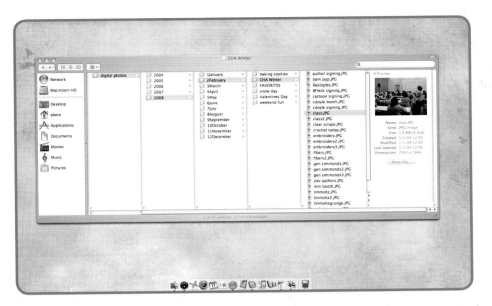

⌃ MasterSolution

Basically, there are two ways to organize photos on your hard drive—by date or by theme. How you scrapbook will give you the answer. If you tend to scrapbook chronologically (or if you remember things according to when they happened), the date method is for you. If you scrapbook as the spirit moves you (or if all those family reunions are blended together in your memory), you may want to go with theme. If you choose to organize by date, create a master folder for at-a-glance management. Inside that, create a folder for each month, and inside those, create folder for each event or activity. Otherwise, organize everything by topic (2008 kids' birthdays, 2008 family reunion, 2008 summer vacation, etc.) or even by group (family events, friends, pets, etc.).

⌄ MasterSolution

Burn, baby, burn! Photo inferno! When it comes to storing digital files, the Masters will tell you to: a) invest in a DVD burner and b) get your bad self some image-organizing software that allows you to print a contact sheet or image index. Why a DVD burner? Because DVDs have a lot more storage capacity than CDs do. The money, time and space you will save in CDs alone could rationalize the cost. With your cool software, you can print out a contact sheet to keep with each DVD. Organization at a glance. Woo hoo!

ExpertAdvice!

From now on (really, I promise), what can I do on a regular basis to streamline the organization of my digital files?

- Edit as you go. When Michele Skinner uploads images to her computer, she immediately goes through them and deletes any that are blurry, bad or repetitive. This saves space on your hard drive and cuts down on time spent looking through everything again and again later.
- Single out your favorites. Amelia McIvor creates a "best of" folder within each category so that she can quickly reference her favorite images from an event or trip. Hillary Heidelberg uses an image-organization program (Picasa) that allows her to star the photos she wants to flag for future use.
- Back it up. All the Masters can't emphasize this enough: Back up your files on an external hard drive or on DVDs to save yourself the heartbreak of losing precious mementos in a hard drive crash or system meltdown. You can also upload your photos to an online photo site, which allows you to have backups that you can access from anywhere and gives you the ability to share them.

Curious: How do you organize your printed photos? Mine are in piles.

First, kudos for actually printing your digital photos. So many digital camera owners neglect to actually print their images, being satisfied with simply viewing them on their computer screen. On the other hand, many scrapbookers would be wise to limit the number of prints they turn out. Digital cameras make it so easy to snap countless images, we often print variations of the same image. To find a happy medium, try to be discriminating with the images you print (plus, it's more environmentally friendly and cost-efficient). Then, once they're printed, be diligent about organizing them. Several ways exist, and our Masters share a few.

⌃ **Master**Solution

Photo albums are great for organizing photos! Well, duh. But, they can be a big, honkin' nightmare—the bigger albums are space hogs and kind of clumsy. Many of the Masters favor their dainty cousin: the mini album. These can make organization a snap as you can dedicate one album to one event or theme, and they have that portability thing going for them should you want to take them to a crop or to share with friends over lunch. (Plus, have you noticed that everything is just cuter when it's mini?)

MasterSolution ≫

The photo box is of course an option, but it will only work if you take the time to sort your photos into envelopes and label them with the theme and date. Otherwise, you may as well just dump your prints in a shoe box and slide them under the bed. A variation on this idea would be to store your images in hanging file folders inside a desk drawer or file cabinet. Again, scrappers, labeling holds the key to your sanity.

The Funny Thing You Said

by Nic Howard

Good ol' 4" × 6" (10cm × 15cm) photos—such a convenient size to have printed, and a great size to use on your layouts, too. Overlay the photos for interest, as Nic does here, and zoom in to capture those cute expressions.

Supplies: Cardstock; patterned paper (Making Memories); rub-ons (American Crafts, BasicGrey, Creative Imaginations, Fancy Pants); letter stickers (Adornit); title card (My Mind's Eye); felt (Queen & Co.)

I've heard several methods for organizing digital kits. Which do you prefer?

A digital scrapbooking kit is like a virtual version of a paper kit. When organizing them, you've gotta figure out what works for you. (Are you noticing a theme here?) When organizing a traditional paper scrapbooking kit, would you keep all of the kit elements together, or would you incorporate the components into your overall system? Keeping kits together insures matching elements are ready to go, but if you're not a matchy-matchy sorta gal, that could present problems. Organize your hard drive in a way that mirrors your scrap space. Tip: You can also copy each of your digital elements so you can store the original set together as a kit and store the duplicates according to page element for the best of both virtual worlds.

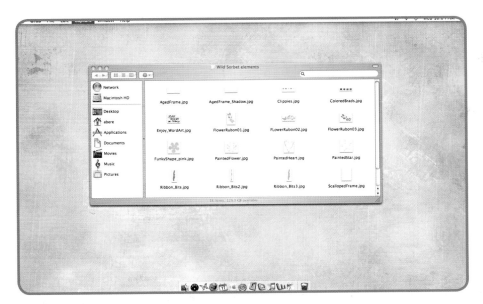

《 Master Solution

All digital kits will have preview images. To view them, head to the kit's preferences menu and choose the option that allows you to view the kit contents as thumbnails. This way, you can see all your available design options at a glance.

《 Master Solution

Even the most digital of scrapbookers can benefit from having a set of digital-kit hard copies. Digital scrapping Masters like Jessie Baldwin and Caroline Ikeji always print out contact sheets of each kit for easy reference. Keep these in a binder and organize them in a way that makes sense to you. Crystal Jeffrey Rieger prefers to file them by designer, for instance. Keep it handy at your computer desk and you can browse through your digital files without even booting up.

My Absolutely Incredible Kid
by Susan Cyrus

Susan's fondness for the digital world of scrapbooking shines through in this layout that uses elements from a couple of different kits. Have fun mixing and matching your digital elements, just like you do your traditional supplies.

Supplies: Digital page kit by Gina Cabrera and Heather Ann Melzer (Digital Design Essentials and Heath Ann Designs collaboration); Misc: Arial Narrow and Susie's Hand fonts

? My digital scrap stash is getting a little out of control with all the fonts, papers and accents. How can I make it less chaotic?

We've talked and talked about organizational systems, and no matter if you're working with paper supplies or digital, the principles are the same. There's no need to reinvent the wheel when you go digital. In fact, you'll make life easier if you don't. Really, by now, you should have a darn good idea as to how you are going to make it happen. What follows are some sweet tips to make your digital designer's corner a bit more streamlined.

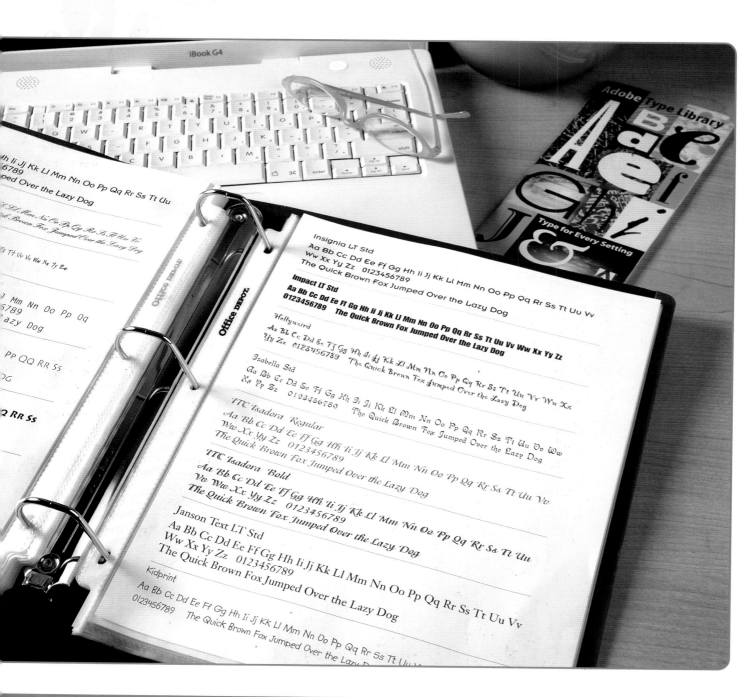

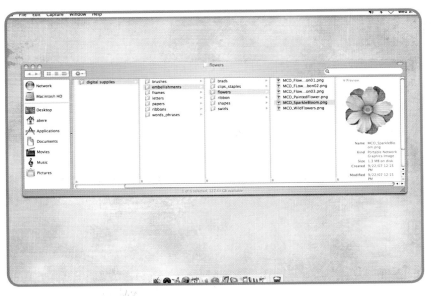

« **Master**Solution

We've said it once, we'll say it again: When organizing digital papers, embellishments and other supplies, mirror the organizational system you have adopted for your traditional supplies. Do you organize paper by color or by manufacturer in your studio? If you organize by color, stick with that system (you can even change the colors of your storage folders to match). One thing you may want to keep in mind is that everything in digital is fluid because you can alter your files (for example, if you downloaded a patterned paper in blue, you can change the color—that's part of the fun). That said, just be sure to maximize your digital stash by maintaining the integrity of those master files if you're creating variations.

« **Master**Solution

Fonts are fun, but trying to find just the right one can be a pain in the bazooti. The standard way requires one to highlight a word and convert it to a million different fonts before finding "the one." The new and improved way, courtesy of the Masters, requires you to print out all of your fonts and organize them into a binder. What a cool option for all your digital (and traditional) scrapbooking needs. Your next perfectly designed title or journaling block is just a flip through the binder away.

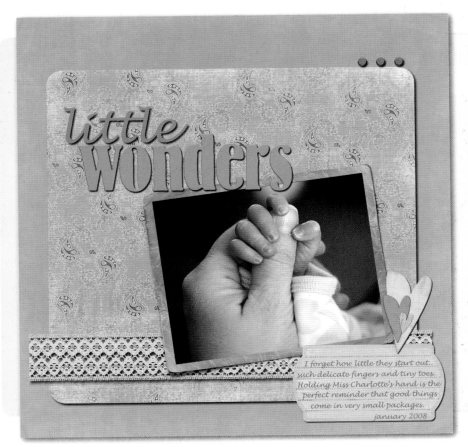

Little Wonders
by Katrina Simeck

If you haven't taken the digital plunge because you don't think you can get the same look as you can with traditional scrapping, allow Katrina to submit this layout for your consideration. Lace, textured cardstock, brads—all these digital elements look good enough to reach out and touch!

Supplies: Digital cardstock by Mindy Terasawa (Designer Digitals); lace, letters by Gina Cabrera (Digital Design Essentials); brads (Shabby Shoppe); chipboard heart, patterned paper, tag (Jen Wilson Designs); frame by Katie Pertiet (Designer Digitals)

How can I display my scraptastic digital layouts? Conversely, how can I digitize my traditional paper layouts?

Digital scrapbookers can take full advantage of the medium by uploading their pages to blogs, Web sites and online galleries, and even e-mailing them to friends and family. Not to be left out, of course, they also can display their layouts just like traditional scrapbookers. Just print them onto the cardstock of choice and frame them, hang them, place them in albums, use them to create calendars, reduce them to wallet size—the sky's the limit. Conversely, you might also belong to the clever sect of scrapbookers who scan their paper layouts for their records and share them electronically with family and friends. You really can have your cake and eat it, too!

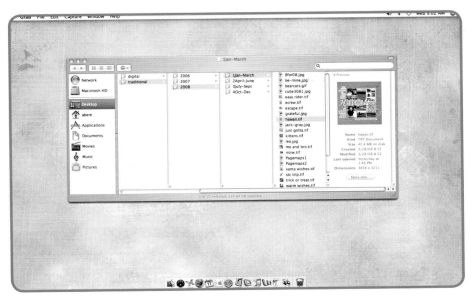

« Master Solution

When you organize your digital layouts, whether you create them 100 percent on the computer or you scan your paper layouts, use the same method that you use to organize your digital photos: date and theme, date and theme, date and theme. Did we mention date and theme? Once you have them all filed and labeled, consider using an image-editing or image-sharing software program or Web site to make a digital slideshow of your layouts. It's a great way to display them on screen.

« Master Solution

Digital layouts, like digital photos, run the risk of being left on the hard drive and going unappreciated. Why not print them? Come on, they deserve a little recognition! These files are digital, so you have the option of printing them any size you want—full size or larger to display in the home, or save a tree and reduce them to make mini albums. You can also punch the corners and thread them on binder rings (those shown here are 6" × 6" [15cm × 15cm]). You can also use these minis as covers for your binders of digital kits or fonts. This is a fun way to display scans of paper layouts, too, without putting the layouts themselves where they can be damaged.

Floatin' Frogs

by Tracie Radtke

Once your photos are organized and easy to find, you might just be inspired to look at them differently, like as a background for the whole layout. With a few other digital elements strategically placed around the main image, Tracie created a layout that really tells a story.

Supplies: Digital Kraft paper by Two Sisters Designs (We Are Storytellers); notebook paper by Amy Martin (Lilypad); circle, green letters by Lisa Whitney (ScrapArtist); buttons, tab by Lauren Reid (Oscraps); black letters, photo corners by Kim Christensen (Prima); brushes (Misprinted Type); Misc: AL Old Remington and Worn Machine fonts

Chapter Five | Masters Gallery

If you are reading this page, there is no doubt you are ready to reinvent your scrap space. This gallery is a little treat for your open-mindedness, a reward for taking the first step toward a more efficient, more organized you. Plus, all the hard work it takes to get organized can leave your creative well in need of refreshment. After all, no book from the Masters would be complete without devoting a few extra pages to what they do best. Think of it as a little extra inspiration to get your creative juices flowing. We hope you've poured yourself a mug of something yummy, because when you turn the page, you're going to cozy up to some exquisitely innovative scrapbook pages from your favorite scrapbook artists.

« **Puppy Moment**
by Nic Howard

When your patterned paper is in order, adding dimension to a layout is a breeze. Just select and layer complementary patterns and textures to create visual interest that isn't too bulky. And by using the measurements on your paper trimmer—a tool Nic always has at the ready—you can easily get the sizes of each layer just right.

Supplies: Patterned paper (Crate Paper, My Mind's Eye); chipboard letters (BasicGrey, CherryArte); rub-ons (BasicGrey); buttons (Autumn Leaves); circle cutter (Accucut); paper trimmer (Fiskars); Misc: 2Peas Hot Chocolate font, paint, thread

Me and My Bro »
by Jodi Amidei

Here's another great idea for using those old CD and DVD cases: Store your die-cut texture plates in them. The plates are flat, so they fit perfectly. When you use these plates, ink the raised portions a bit for even more texture and dimension. Then use them on a standout layout like Jodi's.

Supplies: Cardstock; patterned paper (K&Co.); die-cut machine, letter dies (Spellbinders); embossing plates (Provo Craft); ribbon (Hobby Lobby); Misc: buckles

≪ The Eyes Have It
by Kathy Fesmire

For Kathy, storing chipboard is all about what's most handy. And for her, that means keeping them in a clear garbage can. What could be easier to rifle through to find the perfect letters and shapes for a pretty layout like this?

Supplies: Patterned paper (K&Co., My Mind's Eye); chipboard flowers, flocked brad (Crafts Etc.); chipboard letters (EK Success); ribbon (Offray, Wrights); scalloped accent (Keller's Creations); stamps (Savvy Stamps); Misc: buttons, chipboard tag, ink, paint

Stay Free & Wild ≫
by Staci Etheridge

Staci pulled the black marker used in this layout from her vintage suitcase, pictured on page 29 in the upper right of her cabinet. To re-create this look, draw the large circular scribble, cut it out, then embellish with glitter glue at the intersections.

Supplies: Patterned paper (Around the Block, KI Memories, My Mind's Eye, Zsiage); letter stamps (KI Memories); sticker accents (Doodlebug, KI Memories); labels (Dymo); pens (Sharpie); Misc: glitter glue, notebook paper

≪ Ski Trip
by Diana Graham

One of Diana's storage solutions is to use the pockets of a shoe organizer for her tools and supplies. And that's where she found these tinted ghost letters. Placing them over different patterned papers gives each letter a unique look.

Supplies: Patterned paper (BasicGrey, Creative Imaginations); circle, crown and snowflake accents, decorative tape, photo corner, transparent letters (Heidi Swapp); journaling paper (Making Memories); rhinestones (My Mind's Eye)

≪ Just Gotta Smile

by Angelia Wigginton

Angelia is a real pro at packing for a crop—she's all about the page kits. For the kit used to create this page, she assembled coordinating product from a few manufacturers. Place it all in a baggie, and you're ready to go!

Supplies: Cardstock; patterned paper (Creative Imaginations, Me & My Big Ideas); letter stickers (American Crafts); brads (Doodlebug); rhinestones, rub-ons, sticker accents (Me & My Big Ideas); Misc: Arial Black font

The Cutest Girl ≫

by Iris Babao Uy

Iris has a terrific storage solution for her fibers—spice jars, pictured on page 79—that enables her to quickly find the perfect pieces for her layouts. Here, fringed fibers close the envelope housing the hidden journaling, while other fancy fibers make a beautiful addition to the flower motif.

Supplies: Cardstock; patterned paper (7gypsies, Scenic Route, We R Memory Keepers); rub-ons (Heidi Grace); snaps (We R Memory Keepers); sticker accents (7gypsies, Daisy D's); fibers (BasicGrey); clip (7gypsies); brads (Making Memories); Misc: envelope, rhinestones

The Sweetest
by Kelly Goree

Yummy, yummy chipboard. You just can't get too much. Chipboard shapes, like the cute hearts Kelly used here, can be stored just like your chipboard alphas. Check out the ideas on page 69, then put all that chipboard to use and have fun playing!

Supplies: Cardstock; scalloped cardstock (Bazzill); patterned paper (Making Memories, Scenic Route); chipboard letters (Doodlebug); chipboard hearts (Doodlebug, Heidi Swapp); brad (Queen & Co.); Misc: ink

I Do All My Own Stunts »
by Sheila Doherty

When using chipboard letters and accents, don't forget the negatives—the die-cut space around the shapes you've already used. Here Sheila trimmed out the negative of a chipboard error to nicely accent this energetic page.

Supplies: Cardstock; patterned paper (American Crafts, My Mind's Eye); brads (American Crafts, Making Memories); chipboard arrow (Heidi Swapp); Misc: 2Peas Weathered Fence and Impact fonts

One Last Shot
by Katrina Simeck

Another Master who uses a hanging shoe holder for her chipboard, Katrina easily found the pefect letters for this layout. Their clean black style give a finality that complements the theme of one last photo.

Supplies: Cardstock; patterned paper (BasicGrey); chipboard letters (American Crafts); chipboard accents (Scenic Route); brads (Jo-Ann's)

«« Miss You Grandma
by Jessie Baldwin

Jessie rooted around her lunch box of random fun stuff, pictured on page 33, for the embellishments on this page. Keep a few miscellaneous supplies within sight as you're working—you never know when they'll inspire you.

Supplies: Cardstock; patterned paper (Collage Press, KI Memories, Sweetwater); brads (Bazzill); decorative tape (7gypsies); photo corners (Heidi Swapp)

Queen of the Highway »»
by Ronee Parsons

The collage look of this pretty decoration comes in part through Ronee's use of an old sewing pattern for her background. It's just one of the many supplies she keeps within reach for when inspiration strikes.

Supplies: Canvas (Canvas Concepts); patterned paper (Dove of the East); sewing pattern (McCall); rub-on (BasicGrey); stamps (Purple Onion); Misc: beeswax, paint

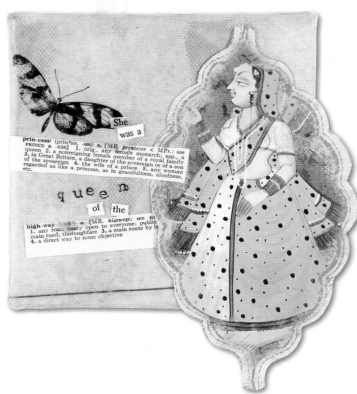

«« Smile
by Valerie Barton

Valerie organizes her fibers by color, so when she was looking for embellishments to tie together her black, white and green color scheme, her stash of green fibers came in awfully handy.

Supplies: Cardstock; patterned paper (KI Memories, My Mind's Eye, Rhonna Designs); metal accents (Die Cuts With A View); fibers (EK Success); rub-ons (Autumn Leaves); Misc: pen, staples

◀◀ I Believe
by Lisa Pace

Lisa's love of the warmth of stitching makes it a necessity to keep her sewing machine right on her desk next to her work area. In this layout, gold thread around the edges helps form a border for the viewer's eye and ties in nicely with the sparkly gold letters.

Supplies: Cardstock; patterned paper (Daisy D's, Making Memories); chipboard letters and shapes (Maya Road); glitter (EK Success); rhinestones (Advantus, Darice); ribbon (Maya Road); die-cut shapes (Ellison); thread (Coats & Clark, Guterman); Misc: Times New Roman font, crystal lacquer, decorative scissors, ink, paint, sequins

DLM Jr. ▶▶
by Ronee Parsons

One of the beauties of digial fonts is they allow you to easily unify the visuals on your layouts. Here, Ronee uses one of the fonts from her title in her journaling. Easy and effective!

Supplies: Digital background paper (Leah Riordan); embellishments by Vicki Stegall (Oscraps)

◀◀ 4th of July
by Jeniece Higgins

Embroidery floss is just one more excellent fiber to have at the ready. Here, Jeniece uses the full six strands to attach chipboard stars to the background paper. Reduce bulk on the back of the layout by taping down the loose ends rather than tying them.

Supplies: Cardstock; bottle cap, wooden letters (Li'l Davis); chipboard stars, ledger paper (Making Memories); wooden tag (Go West); Misc: floss, patterned paper

≪ Falling for You
by Susan Weinroth

By keeping her decorative scissors easily accessible on her central supply rack, Susan can create layered borders in a wink. Combine borders with different edges for maximum effect.

Supplies: Cardstock; patterned paper (KI Memories); letter stickers (American Crafts); metal heart and word stickers, rub-on border (Heidi Grace); decorative scissors, paper punches (Fiskars); Misc: Century Gothic font

Togetherness ≫
by Greta Hammond

Greta keeps her digital die-cut machine on a rolling TV cart which she stores under her worktable. The cartridges fit nicely on the cart's bottom shelf, so she can just grab what she needs as she's creating a layout like this one.

Supplies: Cardstock; chipboard accents, patterned paper, rhinestones, ribbon, rub-ons (Deja Views); die-cut shapes (Provo Craft); digital frame by Rhonna Farrer (Two Peas in a Bucket); Misc: Bradley Hand font, ink

Northwest Rankin »

Northwest Rankin »

by Valerie Barton

Valerie found just the right mix of patterned paper pieces to create the background for this layout. While she used an assortment of scraps from one manufacturer, by sorting your stash by color, you can easily achieve the same effect with a whole mix of papers.

Supplies: Cardstock; patterned paper (My Mind's Eye); metal tag (Stamping Station); rub-on numbers (Making Memories)

« True Love

by Iris Babao Uy

Thanks to her open storage, pictured on pages 29 and 93, Iris' glitter couldn't be more accessible. Because she's the type of scrapper to get inspiration from patterns and colors, having her rainbow of glitter on display keeps all of her sparkly options at a glance.

Supplies: Embossed cardstock, frame, patterned paper (KI Memories); glitter (Doodlebug, Ranger); ribbon (Maya Road, unknown); journaling tab (Maya Road)

« Totally Cool Boy

by Greta Hammond

For this layout, Greta used supplies from one manufacturer—an easy way to create a cohesive page. Try keeping matching supplies like these together in page kits, so they're convenient for when you have a spare moment to scrap.

Supplies: Patterned paper, brads, decorative tape, sticker accents (Deja Views); Misc: Batik Regular font

‹‹ Now and Forever
by Brittany Laakkonen

There's nothing like finding the ideal rub-on for a layout (and once your rub-ons are organized, that's a lot easier to do!). Here, Brittany found two that, although made by different manufacturers, work together well to support the theme of her page.

Supplies: Patterned paper (Prima, Urban Lily, unknown); rub-ons (Making Memories, Urban Lily); flowers, rhinestone swirls (Prima); digital brush by Chris Ford (Two Peas in a Bucket); Misc: ink

A Photo a Day ››
by Caroline Ikeji

Taking a photo a day is a great way to document your life, but it also requires a good storage solution for your digital photos. Check out the ideas on pages 102 and 103, and you'll be totally set to document your every days.

Supplies: Digital frames and paper by Katie Pertiet; flowers, label and stitching by Lynn Grieveson; letters by Anna Aspnes and Katie Pertiet; sequins by Pattie Knox; file tie by Mindy Teasawa (all from Designer Digitals); Misc: SP Wonderful font

« Elizabeth
by Catherine Feegel-Erhardt

Give mismatched letter stickers a unified look by using the stickers as masks. Adhere them to white cardstock, then paint over the entire page. Let the paint dry (yes, it really needs to be dry), then outline the letter shapes with permanent marker. Carefully peel off the letter stickers to reveal the white cardstock underneath.

Supplies: Cardstock; paint (Plaid, Ranger); stamps (Fancy Pants, Heidi Swapp); letter stickers used as masks (American Crafts, Doodlebug, Heidi Grace, Making Memories, Mrs. Grossman's); journaling tag (Maya Road); Misc: buttons, ink, thread, transparency

You Color My Life »
by Valerie Barton

By sorting her buttons by color, Valerie was able to quickly find the perfect embellishments for this layout. To make it even easier on yourself, hand color the black-and-white background paper to match whatever buttons you've chosen to use.

Supplies: Cardstock; patterned paper (KI Memories); letter stickers (Creative Imagination, Making Memories, Stickabilities); Misc: buttons, colored pencils, pen

«« Love

by Kathy Fesmire

Glitter on a layout about your husband? Why not! Here, Kathy used a coarse black glitter for a dramatic effect. Cover your embellishments, like this arrow, with double-sided tape, then let the glitter fly!

Supplies: Cardstock; die-cut shapes, patterned paper, sticker accents (Scenic Route); number stickers (Karen Foster); red line tape adhesive (Keller's Creations); glitter (Sulyn); Misc: adhesive foam, ink, pens

Just Call Me Jack »»

by Greta Hammond

Greta's adhesive addiction (chronicled on page 59) makes layouts like this one a breeze. Simply choose the best adhesive for each element and get busy gluing.

Supplies: Cardstock; chipboard letters, die-cut shapes, patterned paper (Scenic Route); button (BasicGrey); adhesive (EK Success, Provo Craft, Xyron); Misc: Batik Regular font, paint

«« Monster Trucks

by Sheila Doherty

Since Sheila organizes her digital kits both together and as individual elements, she's able to find what she's looking for whether she's in the mood to match or in the mood to mix. Here, she was in the mixing mood, creating elements of her page from four different sources (plus two more sources for fonts!).

Supplies: Digital paper (Jessica Sprague); ledger brush, sanded overlay by Katie Pertiet (Designer Digitals); circles brush, patterned paper by Sande Krieger (Two Peas in a Bucket); button, staple (Shabby Princess); Misc: Impact, JaneAusten, Rockwell and Ruach fonts

« ## Us
by Brittany Laakkonen

Brittany raided her general supplies box for some key components of this layout: a pen, photo tabs, ink, foam adhesive and sandpaper. Sand your chipboard letter, like Brittany did here, to create a pretty and soft distressed look.

Supplies: Cardstock; chipboard letters (Heidi Swapp, Prima); letter stickers, rub-ons (Mustard Moon); Misc: patterned paper

New York City Favorites »
by Shannon Taylor

With her brushes stored in a pretty vase by her paints, Shannon was able to find one to help her create a graffiti look for this layout. Brush on a patch of acrylic paint in the corner and for the title, then stamp with the same paint in another corner to form a visual triangle.

Supplies: Cardstock; patterned paper (My Mind's Eye); letter stickers (Stickabilities); felt flower and word (Creative Imaginations); paint (Making Memories); chipboard circles (Imagination Project); tag (Li'l Davis); chipboard arrow (Technique Tuesday); stamp (Junkitz); Misc: adhesive foam, floss, pen, vintage flower accent

SourceGuide

The following companies manufacture products featured in this book. Please check your local retailers to find these materials, or go to a company's Web site for the latest product information. In addition, we have made every attempt to properly credit the items mentioned in this book. We apologize to any company that we have listed incorrectly, and we would appreciate hearing from you.

7gypsies
(877) 749-7797
www.sevengypsies.com

AccuCut
(800) 288-1670
www.accucut.com

Adobe Systems Incorporated
(800) 833-6687
www.adobe.com

Adornit/Carolee's Creations
(435) 563-1100
www.adornit.com

Advantus Corp.
(904) 482-0091
www.advantus.com

American Crafts
(801) 226-0747
www.americancrafts.com

Around The Block
(801) 593-1946
www.aroundtheblockproducts.com

Autumn Leaves
(800) 727-2727
www.creativityinc.com

BasicGrey
(801) 544-1116
www.basicgrey.com

Bazzill Basics Paper
(480) 558-8557
www.bazzillbasics.com

Berwick Offray, LLC
(800) 237-9425
www.offray.com

BoBunny Press
(801) 771-4010
www.bobunny.com

Canvas Concepts
(800) 869-7220
www.canvasconcepts.com

Chatterbox, Inc.
(208) 461-5077
www.chatterboxinc.com

CherryArte
(212) 465-3495
www.cherryarte.com

Cloud 9 Design
(866) 348-5661
www.cloud9design.biz

Coats & Clark
(800) 648-1479
www.coatsandclark.com

Collage Press
(435) 676-2039
www.collagepress.com

Cosmo Cricket
(800) 852-8810
www.cosmocricket.com

Crafter's Workshop, The
www.thecraftersworkshop.com

Crafts, Etc. Ltd.
(800) 888-0321 x 1275
www.craftsetc.com

Crate Paper
(801) 798-8996
www.cratepaper.com

Creative Imaginations
(800) 942-6487
www.cigift.com

Creative Impressions Rubber Stamps, Inc.
(719) 596-4860
www.creativeimpressions.com

Daisy D's Paper Company
(888) 601-8955
www.daisydspaper.com

Darice, Inc.
(866) 432-7423
www.darice.com

DecoArt Inc.
(800) 367-3047
www.decoart.com

Dèjá Views/C-Thru Ruler
(800) 243-0303
www.dejaviews.com

Designer Digitals
www.designerdigitals.com

Die Cuts With A View
(801) 224-6766
www.diecutswithaview.com

Digital Design Essentials
www.digitaldesignessentials.com

Doodlebug Design Inc.
(877) 800-9190
www.doodlebug.ws

Dove of the East
www.doveoftheeast.com

Dymo
(800) 426-7827
www.dymo.com

EK Success, Ltd.
www.eksuccess.com

Ellison
(800) 253-2238
www.ellison.com

Fancy Pants Designs, LLC
(801) 779-3212
www.fancypantsdesigns.com

Fiskars, Inc.
(866) 348-5661
www.fiskars.com

Frances Meyer, Inc.
(413) 584-5446
www.francesmeyer.com

Go West Studios
www.goweststudios.com

Gutermann
www.gutermann.com

Hambly Screenprints
(800) 707-0977
www.hamblyscreenprints.com

Heather Ann Designs
www.heatheranndesigns.com

Heidi Grace Designs, Inc.
(866) 347-5277
www.heidigrace.com

Heidi Swapp/Advantus Corporation
(904) 482-0092
www.heidiswapp.com

Hero Arts Rubber Stamps, Inc.
(800) 822-4376
www.heroarts.com

Hobby Lobby Stores, Inc.
www.hobbylobby.com

Hot Off The Press, Inc.
(800) 227-9595
www.b2b.hotp.com

Imagination Project, Inc.
www.imaginationproject.com

Jen Wilson Designs
www.jenwilsondesigns.com

Jessica Sprague
www.jessicasprague.com

Jo-Ann Stores
www.joann.com

Junkitz - no longer in business

K&Company
(888) 244-2083
www.kandcompany.com

Karen Foster Design
(801) 451-9779
www.karenfosterdesign.com

Keller's Creations
(803) 279-1779
www.acidfree.com

KI Memories
(972) 243-5595
www.kimemories.com

Lazar Studiowerx, Inc.
(866) 478-9379
www.lazarstudiowerx.com

Li'l Davis Designs
(480) 223-0080
www.lildavisdesigns.com

LilyPad, The
www.the-lilypad.com

Ma Vinci's Reliquary
www.reliquary.cyberstampers.com

Making Memories
(801) 294-0430
www.makingmemories.com

Martha Stewart Crafts
www.marthastewartcrafts.com

Maya Road, LLC
(877) 427-7764
www.mayaroad.com

McCall Pattern Co., The
(800) 766-3619
www.mccall.com

McGill, Inc.
(800) 982-9884
www.mcgillinc.com

Me & My Big Ideas
(949) 583-2065
www.meandmybigideas.com

Melissa Frances/Heart & Home, Inc.
(888) 616-6166
www.melissafrances.com

Misprinted Type
www.misprinted.com

Mrs. Grossman's Paper
Company
(800) 429-4549
www.mrsgrossmans.com

Mustard Moon
(763) 493-5157
www.mustardmoon.com

My Mind's Eye, Inc.
(800) 665-5116
www.mymindseye.com

Offray- see Berwick Offray, LLC

Oscraps
www.oscraps.com

Paper Source
(888) 727-3711
www.paper-source.com

Paper Studio
(480) 557-5700
www.paperstudio.com

Plaid Enterprises, Inc.
(800) 842-4197
www.plaidonline.com

Prima Marketing, Inc.
(909) 627-5532
www.primamarketinginc.com

Provo Craft
(800) 937-7686
www.provocraft.com

Purple Onion Designs
www.purpleoniondesigns.com

Queen & Co.
(858) 613-7858
www.queenandcompany.com

QuicKutz, Inc.
(888) 702-1146
www.quickutz.com

Rhonna Designs
www.rhonnadesigns.com

Rubber Cafe, The
(805) 466-2252
www.therubbercafe.com

Sakura Hobby Craft
(310) 212-7878
www.sakuracraft.com

Sandylion Sticker Designs
(800) 387-4215
www.sandylion.com

Sanford Corporation
(800) 323-0749
www.sanfordcorp.com

Sassafras Lass
(801) 269-1331
www.sassafraslass.com

Savvy Stamps
(866) 447-2889
www.savvystamps.com

Scenic Route Paper Co.
(801) 542-8071
www.scenicroutepaper.com

ScrapArtist
(734) 717-7775
www.scrapartist.com

Scrapbook Graphics
www.scrapbookgraphics.com

**Scrapworks, LLC /
As You Wish Products, LLC**
(801) 363-1010
www.scrapworks.com

SEI, Inc.
(800) 333-3279
www.shopsei.com

Shabby Princess
www.shabbyprincess.com

Shabby Shoppe, The
www.theshabbyshoppe.com

Sharpie - see Sanford

Spellbinders Paper Arts, LLC
(888) 547-0400
www.spellbinders.us

Stampabilities
(800) 888-0321
www.stampabilities.com

Stamping Station
(801) 444-3828
www.stampingstation.com

Stickabilities - no source available

Sulyn Industries, Inc.
(954) 755-2311
www.sulyn.com

Sweetwater
(800) 359-3094
www.sweetwaterscrapbook.com

Target
www.target.com

Tattered Angels
(970) 622-9444
www.mytatteredangels.com

Technique Tuesday, LLC
(503) 644-4073
www.techniquetuesday.com

Tim Holtz
www.timholtz.com

Trace Industries - no longer in business

Two Peas in a Bucket
(888) 896-7327
www.twopeasinabucket.com

Urban Lily
www.urbanlily.com

Wal-Mart Stores, Inc.
www.walmart.com

We Are Storytellers
www.wearestorytellers.com

We R Memory Keepers, Inc.
(801) 539-5000
www.weronthenet.com

WorldWin Papers
(888) 834-6455
www.worldwinpapers.com

Wrights Ribbon Accents
(877) 597-4448
www.wrights.com

Xyron
(800) 793-3523
www.xyron.com

Zsiage, LLC
(718) 224-1976
www.zsiage.com

Index

Get more scrapbooking ideas from
Memory Makers Masters!

« Ask the Masters!

Learn innovative techniques and solutions from the Memory Makers Masters for creating flawless scrapbook pages.

ISBN-13: 978-1-892127-88-4
ISBN-10: 1-892127-88-1
paperback
128 pages
Z0277

» Ask the Masters! Making the Most of Your Scrapbook Supplies

This book is filled with innovative and inspiring ideas from the Memory Makers Masters for using that growing stash of scrapbook supplies and tools.

ISBN-13: 978-1-59963-012-0
ISBN-10: 1-59963-012-5
paperback
128 pages
Z1040

« Scrap Simple

Scrapbooking doesn't have to be fussy to be fun! Scrap Simple makes it easy to whip up clean and uncluttered scrapbook pages in a flash.

ISBN-13: 978-1-59963-014-4
ISBN-10: 1-59963-014-1
paperback
128 pages
Z1282

» Cut Loose: Break the Rules of Scrapbooking

Life is full of rules–and scrapbooking is no exception. Cut Loose shows you how to break free from the confines of typical scrapbooking and breathe new life into your pages.

ISBN-13: 978-1-59963-020-5
ISBN-10: 1-59963-020-6
Paperback
128 pages
Z1806

These books and other fine Memory Makers titles are available at your local scrapbook or craft store, bookstore or from online suppliers. Visit our Web sites at **www.mycraftivity.com** and **www.memorymakersmagazine.com**

See what's coming up from Memory Makers Books by checking out our blog:
www.mycraftivity.com/scrapbooking_papercrafts/blog/